ampson County Unit of the   NORTH CAROLINA
Vayne Technical Institute   STATE BOARD OF EDUCATION
. O. Drawer 855   DEPT. OF COMMUNITY COLLEGES
linton, North Carolina   28328

PENGUIN BOOKS

PL1

CÆSAR AND CLEOPATRA

BERNARD SHAW

AR AND CLEOPATRA

A HISTORY

BY

BERNARD SHAW

PENGUIN BOOKS

BALTIMORE · MARYLAND

This edition first published April 1951
Reprinted 1957, 1959, 1960, 1962, 1966

Penguin Books Inc.

3300 Clipper Mill Road, Baltimore, Maryland 21211

Printed in the United States of America

Contents

CÆSAR AND CLEOPATRA

PROLOGUE

In the doorway of the temple of Ra in Memphis. Deep gloom. An august personage with a hawk's head is mysteriously visible by his own light in the darkness within the temple. He surveys the modern audience with great contempt; and finally speaks the following words to them.

Peace! Be silent and hearken unto me, ye quaint little islanders. Give ear, ye men with white paper on your breasts and nothing written thereon (to signify the innocency of your minds). Hear me, ye women who adorn yourselves alluringly and conceal your thoughts from your men, leading them to believe that ye deem them wondrous strong and masterful whilst in truth ye hold them in your hearts as children without judgment. Look upon my hawk's head; and know that I am Ra, who was once in Egypt a mighty god. Ye cannot kneel nor prostrate yourselves; for ye are packed in rows without freedom to move, obstructing one another's vision; neither do any of ye regard it as seemly to do aught until ye see all the rest do so too; wherefore it commonly happens that in great emergencies ye do nothing, though each telleth his fellow that something must be done. I ask you not for worship, but for silence. Let not your men speak nor your women cough; for I am come to draw you back two thousand years over the graves of sixty generations. Ye poor posterity, think not that ye are the first. Other fools before ye have seen the sun rise and set, and the moon change her shape and her hour. As they were so ye are; and yet not so great; for the pyramids my people built stand to this day; whilst the dustheaps on which ye slave, and which ye call empires, scatter in the wind even as ye pile your dead sons' bodies on them to make yet more dust.

Hearken to me then, oh ye compulsorily educated ones. Know that even as there is an old England and a new, and ye stand perplexed between the twain; so in the days when I was worshipped was there an old Rome and a new, and men standing perplexed between them. And the old Rome was poor and little, and greedy and fierce, and evil in many ways; but because its mind was little and its work was simple, it knew its own mind and did its own work; and the gods pitied it and helped it and strengthened it and shielded it; for the gods are patient with littleness. Then the old Rome, like the beggar on horseback, presumed on the favor of the gods, and said, "Lo! there is neither riches nor greatness in our littleness: the road to riches and greatness is through robbery of the poor and slaughter of the weak." So they robbed their own poor until they became great masters of that art, and knew by what laws it could be made to appear seemly and honest. And when they had squeezed their own poor dry, they robbed the poor of other lands, and added those lands to Rome until there came a new Rome, rich and huge. And I, Ra, laughed; for the minds of the Romans remained the same size whilst their dominion spread over the earth.

Now mark me, that ye may understand what ye are presently to see. Whilst the Romans still stood between the old Rome and the new, there arose among them a mighty soldier: Pompey the Great. And the way of the soldier is the way of death; but the way of the gods is the way of life; and so it comes that a god at the end of his way is wise and a soldier at the end of his way is a fool. So Pompey held by the old Rome, in which only soldiers could become great; but the gods turned to the new Rome, in which any man with wit enough could become what he would. And Pompey's friend Julius Cæsar was on the side of the gods; for he saw that Rome had passed beyond the control of the little old Romans. This Cæsar was a great talker and a politician: he bought men with words and with gold, even as ye are bought. And when they would not be satisfied with words and gold, and demanded also the glories of war, Cæsar in his middle age turned his hand to that trade; and they that were against him when he sought their welfare, bowed down before him when he became a slayer and a conqueror; for such is the nature of you mortals. And as for Pompey, the gods grew tired of his triumphs and his airs of being himself a god; for he talked of law and duty and other matters that concerned not a mere human worm. And the gods smiled on Cæsar; for he lived the life they had given him boldly, and was not forever rebuking us for our indecent ways of creation, and hiding our handiwork as a shameful thing. Ye know well what I mean; for this is one of your own sins.

And thus it fell out between the old Rome and the new, that Cæsar said, "Unless I break the law of old Rome, I cannot take my share in ruling her; and the gift of ruling that the gods gave me will perish without fruit." But Pompey said, "The law is above all; and if thou break it thou shalt die." Then said Cæsar, "I will break it: kill me who can." And he broke it. And Pompey went for him, as ye say, with a great army to slay him and uphold the old Rome. So Cæsar fled across the Adriatic sea; for the high gods had a lesson to teach him, which lesson they shall also teach you in due time if ye continue to forget them and to worship that cad among gods, Mammon. Therefore before they raised Cæsar to be master of the world, they were minded to throw him down into the dust, even beneath the feet of Pompey, and blacken his face before the nations. And Pompey they raised higher than ever, he and his laws and his high mind that aped the gods, so that his fall might be the more terrible. And Pompey followed Cæsar, and overcame him with all the majesty of old Rome, and stood over him and over the whole world even as ye stand over it with your fleet that covers thirty miles of the sea. And when Cæsar was brought down to utter nothingness, he made a last stand to die honorably, and did not despair; for he said, "Against me there is Pompey, and

the old Rome, and the law and the legions: all all against
me; but high above these are the gods; and Pompey is a
fool." And the gods laughed and approved; and on the field
of Pharsalia the impossible came to pass; the blood and iron
ye pin your faith on fell before the spirit of man; for the
spirit of man is the will of the gods; and Pompey's power
crumbled in his hand, even as the power of imperial Spain
crumbled when it was set against your fathers in the days
when England was little, and knew her own mind, and had
a mind to know instead of a circulation of newspapers.
Wherefore look to it, lest some little people whom ye would
enslave rise up and become in the hand of God the scourge
of your boastings and your injustices and your lusts and
stupidities.

And now, would ye know the end of Pompey, or will ye
sleep while a god speaks? Heed my words well; for Pompey
went where ye are gone, even to Egypt, where there was a
Roman occupation even as there was but now a British one.
And Cæsar pursued Pompey to Egypt: a Roman fleeing, and
a Roman pursuing: dog eating dog. And the Egyptians said,
"Lo: these Romans which have lent money to our kings and
levied a distraint upon us with their arms, call for ever upon
us to be loyal to them by betraying our own country to
them. But now behold two Romes! Pompey's Rome and
Cæsar's Rome! To which of the twain shall we pretend to
be loyal?" So they turned in their perplexity to a soldier that
had once served Pompey, and that knew the way of Rome
and was full of her lusts. And they said to him, "Lo: in thy
country dog eats dog; and both dogs are coming to eat us:
what counsel hast thou to give us?" And this soldier, whose
name was Lucius Septimius, and whom ye shall presently
see before ye, replied, "Ye shall diligently consider which is
the bigger dog of the two; and ye shall kill the other dog for
his sake and thereby earn his favor." And the Egyptians
said, "Thy counsel is expedient; but if we kill a man outside
the law we set ourselves in the place of the gods; and this we

dare not do. But thou, being a Roman, art accustomed to this kind of killing; for thou hast imperial instincts. Wilt thou therefore kill the lesser dog for us?" And he said, "I will; for I have made my home in Egypt; and I desire consideration and influence among you." And they said, "We knew well thou wouldst not do it for nothing: thou shalt have thy reward." Now when Pompey came, he came alone in a little galley, putting his trust in the law and the constitution. And it was plain to the people of Egypt that Pompey was now but a very small dog. So when he set his foot on the shore he was greeted by his old comrade Lucius Septimius, who welcomed him with one hand and with the other smote off his head, and kept it as it were a pickled cabbage to make a present to Cæsar. And mankind shuddered; but the gods laughed; for Septimius was but a knife that Pompey had sharpened; and when it turned against his own throat they said that Pompey had better have made Septimius a ploughman than so brave and readyhanded a slayer. Therefore again I bid you beware, ye who would all be Pompeys if ye dared; for war is a wolf that may come to your own door.

Are ye impatient with me? Do ye crave for a story of an unchaste woman? Hath the name of Cleopatra tempted ye hither? Ye foolish ones; Cleopatra is as yet but a child that is whipped by her nurse. And what I am about to shew you for the good of your souls is how Cæsar, seeking Pompey in Egypt, found Cleopatra; and how he received that present of a pickled cabbage that was once the head of Pompey; and what things happened between the old Cæsar and the child queen before he left Egypt and battled his way back to Rome to be slain there as Pompey was slain, by men in whom the spirit of Pompey still lived. All this ye shall see; and ye shall marvel, after your ignorant manner, that men twenty centuries ago were already just such as you, and spoke and lived as ye speak and live, no worse and no better, no wiser and no sillier. And the two thousand years that have past are to me, the god Ra, but a moment; nor is this day any other than the day in which Cæsar set foot in the land of my people. And now I leave you; for ye are a dull folk, and instruction is wasted on you; and I had not spoken so much but that it is in the nature of a god to struggle for ever with the dust and the darkness, and to drag from them, by the force of his longing for the divine, more life and more light. Settle ye therefore in your seats and keep silent; for ye are about to hear a man speak, and a great man he was, as ye count greatness. And fear not that I shall speak to you again: the rest of the story must ye learn from them that lived it. Farewell; and do not presume to applaud me. [*The temple vanishes in utter darkness*].

[1912]

AN ALTERNATIVE TO THE PROLOGUE

An October night on the Syrian border of Egypt towards the end of the XXXIII Dynasty, in the year 706 by Roman computation, afterwards reckoned by Christian computation as 48 B.C. A great radiance of silver fire, the dawn of a moonlit night, is rising in the east. The stars and the cloudless sky are our own contemporaries, nineteen and a half centuries younger than we know them; but you would not guess that from their appearance. Below them are two notable drawbacks of civilization: a palace, and soldiers. The palace, an old, low, Syrian building of whitened mud, is not so ugly as Buckingham Palace; and the officers in the courtyard are more highly civilized than modern English officers: for example, they do not dig up the corpses of their dead enemies and mutilate them, as we dug up Cromwell and the Mahdi. They are in two groups: one intent on the gambling of their captain Belzanor, a warrior of fifty, who, with his spear on the ground beside his knee, is stooping to throw dice with a sly-looking young Persian recruit; the other gathered about a guardsman who has just finished telling a naughty story (still current in English barracks) at which they are laughing uproariously. They are about a dozen in number, all highly aristocratic young Egyptian guardsmen, handsomely equipped with weapons and armor, very unEnglish in point of not being ashamed of and uncomfortable in their professional dress; on the contrary, rather ostentatiously and arrogantly warlike, as valuing themselves on their military caste.

Belzanor is a typical veteran, tough and wilful; prompt, capable and crafty where brute force will serve; helpless and boyish when it will not: an active sergeant, an incompetent general, a deplorable dictator. Would, if influentially connected, be employed in the two last capacities by a modern European State on the strength of his success in the first. Is rather to be pitied just now in view of the fact that Julius Cæsar is invading his country. Not knowing this, is intent on his game with the Persian, whom, as a foreigner, he considers quite capable of cheating him.

His subalterns are mostly handsome young fellows whose interest in the game and the story symbolize with tolerable completeness the main interests in life of which they are conscious. Their spears are leaning against the walls, or lying on the ground ready to their hands. The corner of the courtyard forms a triangle of which one side is the front of the palace, with a doorway, the other a wall with a gateway. The storytellers are on the palace side: the gamblers, on the gateway side. Close to the gateway, against the wall, is a stone block high enough to enable a Nubian sentinel, standing on it, to look over the wall. The yard is lighted by a torch stuck in the wall. As the laughter from the group round the storyteller dies away, the kneeling Persian, winning the throw, snatches up the stake from the ground.

BELZANOR. By Apis, Persian, thy gods are good to thee.

THE PERSIAN. Try yet again, O captain. Double or quits!

BELZANOR. No more. I am not in the vein.

THE SETINEL [*poising his javelin as he peers over the wall*] Stand. Who goes there?

They all start, listening. A strange voice replies from without.

VOICE. The bearer of evil tidings.

BELZANOR [*calling to the sentry*] Pass him.

THE SENTINEL [*grounding his javelin*] Draw near, O bearer of evil tidings.

BELZANOR [*pocketing the dice and picking up his spear*] Let us receive this man with honor. He bears evil tidings.

The guardsmen seize their spears and gather about the gate, leaving a way through for the new comer.

PERSIAN [*rising from his knee*] Are evil tidings, then, so honorable?

BELZANOR. O barbarous Persian, hear my instruction. In Egypt the bearer of good tidings is sacrificed to the gods as a thank offering; but no god will accept the blood of the messenger of evil. When we have good tidings, we are careful to send them in the mouth of the cheapest slave we can find. Evil tidings are borne by young noblemen who desire to bring themselves into notice. [*They join the rest at the gate*].

THE SENTINEL. Pass. O young captain; and bow the head in the House of the Queen.

VOICE. Go anoint thy javelin with fat of swine, O Blackamoor: for before morning the Romans will make thee eat it to the very butt.

The owner of the voice, a fairhaired dandy, dressed in a different fashion from that affected by the guardsmen, but no less extravagantly, comes through the gateway laughing. He is somewhat battlestained; and his left forearm, bandaged, comes through a torn sleeve. In his right hand he carries a Roman sword in its sheath. He swaggers down the courtyard, the Persian on his right, Belzanor on his left, and the guardsmen crowding down behind him.

BELZANOR. Who are thou that laughest in the House of Cleopatra the Queen, and in the teeth of Belzanor, the captain of her guard?

THE NEW COMER. I am Bel Affris, descended from the gods.

BELZANOR [*ceremoniously*] Hail, cousin!

ALL [*except the Persian*] Hail, cousin!

PERSIAN. All the Queen's guards are descended from the gods, O stranger, save myself. I am Persian, and descended from many kings.

BEL AFFRIS [*to the guardsmen*] Hail, cousins! [*To the Persian, condescendingly*] Hail, mortal!

BELZANOR. You have been in battle, Bel Affris; and you are a soldier among soldiers. You will not let the Queen's women have the first of your tidings.

BEL AFFRIS. I have no tidings, except that we shall have our throats cut presently, women, soldiers, and all.

PERSIAN [*to Belzanor*] I told you so.

THE SENTINEL [*who has been listening*] Woe, alas!

BEL AFFRIS [*calling to him*] Peace, peace, poor Ethiop: destiny is with the gods who painted thee black. [*To Belzanor*] What has this mortal [*indicating the Persian*] told you?

BELZANOR. He says that the Roman Julius Cæsar, who has landed on our shores with a handful of followers, will make himself master of Egypt. He is afraid of the Roman soldiers. [*The guardsmen laugh with boisterous scorn*]. Peasants, brought up to scare crows and follow the plough! Sons of smiths and millers and tanners! And we nobles, consecrated to arms, descended from the gods!

PERSIAN. Belzanor: the gods are not always good to their poor relations.

BELZANOR [*hotly, to the Persian*] Man to man, are we worse than the slaves of Cæsar?

BEL AFFRIS [*stepping between them*] Listen, cousin. Man to man, we Egyptians are as gods above the Romans.

THE GUARDSMEN [*exultantly*] Aha!

BEL AFFRIS. But this Cæsar does not pit man against man: he throws a legion at you where you are weakest as he throws a stone from a catapult; and that legion is as a man with one head, a thousand arms, and no religion. I have fought against them; and I know.

BELZANOR [*derisively*] Were you frightened, cousin?

The guardsmen roar with laughter, their eyes sparkling at the wit of their captain.

BEL AFFRIS. No, cousin; but I was beaten. They were frightened (perhaps); but they scattered us like chaff.

The guardsmen, much damped, utter a growl of contemptuous disgust.

BELZANOR. Could you not die?

BEL AFFRIS. No: that was too easy to be worthy of a descendant of the gods. Besides, there was no time: all was over in a moment. The attack came just where we least expected it.

BELZANOR. That shews that the Romans are cowards.

BEL AFFRIS. They care nothing about cowardice, these Romans: they fight to win. The pride and honor of war are nothing to them.

PERSIAN. Tell us the tale of the battle. What befell?

THE GUARDSMEN [gathering eagerly round Bel Affris] Ay: the tale of the battle.

BEL AFFRIS. Know then, that I am a novice in the guard of the temple of Ra in Memphis, serving neither Cleopatra nor her brother Ptolemy, but only the high gods. We went a journey to inquire of Ptolemy why he had driven Cleopatra into Syria, and how we of Egypt should deal with the Roman Pompey, newly come to our shores after his defeat by Cæsar at Pharsalia. What, think ye, did we learn? Even that Cæsar is coming also in hot pursuit of his foe, and that Ptolemy has slain Pompey, whose severed head he holds in readiness to present to the conqueror. [Sensation among the guardsmen]. Nay, more: we found that Cæsar is already come; for we had not made half a day's journey on our way back when we came upon a city rabble flying from his legions, whose landing they had gone out to withstand.

BELZANOR. And ye, the temple guard! did ye not withstand these legions?

BEL AFFRIS. What man could, that we did. But there came the sound of a trumpet whose voice was as the cursing of a black mountain. Then saw we a moving wall of shields coming towards us. You know how the heart burns when you charge a fortified wall; but how if the fortified wall were to charge you?

THE PERSIAN [exulting in having told them so] Did I not say it?

BEL AFFRIS. When the wall came nigh, it changed into a line of men—common fellows enough, with helmets, leather tunics, and breastplates. Every man of them flung his javelin:

the one that came my way drove through my shield as through a papyrus—lo there! [*he points to the bandage on his left arm*] and would have gone through my neck had I not stooped. They were charging at the double then, and were upon us with short swords almost as soon as their javelins. When a man is close to you with such a sword, you can do nothing with our weapons: they are all too long.

THE PERSIAN. What did you do?

BEL AFFRIS. Doubled my fist and smote my Roman on the sharpness of his jaw. He was but mortal after all: he lay down in a stupor; and I took his sword and laid it on. [*Drawing the sword*] Lo! a Roman sword with Roman blood on it!

THE GUARDSMEN [*approvingly*] Good! [*They take the sword and hand it round, examining it curiously*].

THE PERSIAN. And your men?

BEL AFFRIS. Fled. Scattered like sheep.

BELZANOR [*furiously*] The cowardly slaves! Leaving the descendants of the gods to be butchered!

BEL AFFRIS [*with acid coolness*] The descendants of the gods did not stay to be butchered, cousin. The battle was not to the strong; but the race was to the swift. The Romans who have no chariots, sent a cloud of horsemen in pursuit, and slew multitudes. Then our high priest's captain rallied a dozen descendants of the gods and exhorted us to die fighting. I said to myself: surely it is safer to stand than to lose my breath and be stabbed in the back; so I joined our captain and stood. Then the Romans treated us with respect; for no man attacks a lion when the field is full of sheep, except for the pride and honor of war, of which these Romans know nothing. So we escaped with our lives; and I am come to warn you that you must open your gates to Cæsar; for his advance guard is scarce an hour behind me; and not an Egyptian warrior is left standing between you and his legions.

THE SENTINEL. Woe, alas! [*He throws down his javelin*

and flies into the palace].

BELZANOR. Nail him to the door, quick! [*The guardsmen rush for him with their spears; but he is too quick for them*]. Now this news will run through the palace like fire through stubble.

BEL AFFRIS. What shall we do to save the women from the Romans?

BELZANOR. Why not kill them?

PERSIAN. Because we should have to pay blood money for some of them. Better let the Romans kill them: it is cheaper.

BELZANOR [*awestruck at his brain power*] O subtle one! O serpent!

BEL AFFRIS. But your Queen?

BELZANOR. True: we must carry off Cleopatra.

BEL AFFRIS. Will ye not await her command?

BELZANOR. Command! a girl of sixteen! Not we. At Memphis ye deem her a Queen: here we know better. I will take her on the crupper of my horse. When we soldiers have carried her out of Cæsar's reach, then the priests and the nurses and the rest of them can pretend she is a queen again, and put their commands into her mouth.

PERSIAN. Listen to me, Belzanor.

BELZANOR. Speak, O subtle beyond thy years.

THE PERSIAN. Cleopatra's brother Ptolemy is at war with her. Let us sell her to him.

THE GUARDSMEN. O subtle one! O serpent!

BELZANOR. We dare not. We are descended from the gods; but Cleopatra is descended from the river Nile; and the lands of our fathers will grow no grain if the Nile rises not to water them. Without our father's gifts we should live the lives of dogs.

PERSIAN. It is true: the Queen's guard cannot live on its pay. But hear me further, O ye kinsmen of Osiris.

THE GUARDSMEN. Speak, O subtle one. Hear the serpent begotten!

PERSIAN. Have I heretofore spoken truly to you of Cæsar,

when you thought I mocked you?

GUARDSMEN. Truly, truly.

BELZANOR [reluctantly admitting it] So Bel Affris says.

PERSIAN. Hear more of him, then. This Cæsar is a great lover of women: he makes them his friends and counsellors.

BELZANOR. Faugh! This rule of women will be the ruin of Egypt.

THE PERSIAN. Let it rather be the ruin of Rome! Cæsar grows old now: he is past fifty and full of labors and battles. He is too old for the young women; and the old women are too wise to worship him.

BEL AFFRIS. Take heed, Persian. Cæsar is by this time almost within earshot.

PERSIAN. Cleopatra is not yet a woman: neither is she wise. But she already troubles men's wisdom.

BELZANOR. Ay: that is because she is descended from the river Nile and a black kitten of the sacred White Cat. What then?

PERSIAN. Why, sell her secretly to Ptolemy, and then offer ourselves to Cæsar as volunteers to fight for the overthrow of her brother and the rescue of our Queen, the Great Granddaughter of the Nile.

THE GUARDSMEN. O serpent!

PERSIAN. He will listen to us if we come with her picture in our mouths. He will conquer and kill her brother, and reign in Egypt with Cleopatra for his Queen. And we shall be her guard.

GUARDSMEN. O subtlest of all the serpents! O admiration! O wisdom!

BEL AFFRIS. He will also have arrived before you have done talking, O word spinner.

BELZANOR. That is true. [An affrighted uproar in the palace interrupts him]. Quick: the flight has begun: guard the door. [They rush to the door and form a cordon before it with their spears. A mob of women-servants and nurses surges out. Those in front recoil from the spears, screaming *to those behind to keep back. Belzanor's voice dominates the disturbance as he shouts*] Back there. In again, unprofitable cattle.

THE GUARDSMEN. Back, unprofitable cattle.

BELZANOR. Send us out Ftatateeta, the Queen's chief nurse.

THE WOMEN [*calling into the palace*] Ftatateeta, Ftatateeta. Come, come. Speak to Belzanor.

A WOMAN. Oh, keep back. You are thrusting me on the spearheads.

A huge grim woman, her face covered with a network of tiny wrinkles, and her eyes old, large, and wise; sinewy handed, very tall, very strong; with the mouth of a bloodhound and the jaws of a bulldog, appears on the threshold. She is dressed like a person of consequence in the palace, and confronts the guardsmen insolently.

FTATATEETA. Make way for the Queen's chief nurse.

BELZANOR [*with solemn arrogance*] Ftatateeta: I am Belzanor, the captain of the Queen's guard, descended from the gods.

FTATATEETA [*retorting his arrogance with interest*] Belzanor: I am Ftatateeta, the Queen's chief nurse; and your divine ancestors were proud to be painted on the wall in the pyramids of the kings whom my fathers served.

The women laugh triumphantly.

BELZANOR [*with grim humor*] Ftatateeta: daughter of a long-tongued, swivel-eyed chameleon, the Romans are at hand. [*A cry of terror from the women: they would fly but for the spears*] Not even the descendants of the gods can resist them; for they have each man seven arms, each carrying seven spears. The blood in their veins is boiling quicksilver; and their wives become mothers in three hours, and are slain and eaten the next day.

A shudder of horror from the women. Ftatateeta, despising them and scorning the soldiers, pushes her way through the crowd and confronts the spear points undismayed.

FTATATEETA. Then fly and save yourselves, O cowardly sons

of the cheap clay gods that are sold to fish porters; and leave us to shift for ourselves.

BELZANOR. Not until you have first done our bidding, O terror of manhood. Bring out Cleopatra the Queen to us; and then go whither you will.

FTATATEETA [*with a derisive laugh*] Now I know why the gods have taken her out of our hands. [*The guardsmen start and look at one another*]. Know, thou foolish soldier, that the Queen has been missing since an hour past sundown.

BELZANOR [*furiously*] Hag: you have hidden her to sell to Cæsar or her brother. [*He grasps her by the left wrist, and drags her, helped by a few of the guard, to the middle of the courtyard, where, as they fling her on her knees, he draws a murderous looking knife*]. Where is she? Where is she? or— [*he threatens to cut her throat*].

FTATATEETA [*savagely*] Touch me, dog; and the Nile will not rise on your fields for seven times seven years of famine.

BELZANOR [*frightened, but desperate*] I will sacrifice: I will pay. Or stay. [*To the Persian*] You, O subtle one: your father's lands lie far from the Nile. Slay her.

PERSIAN [*threatening her with his knife*] Persia has but one god; yet he loves the blood of old women. Where is Cleopatra?

FTATATEETA. Persian: as Osiris lives, I do not know. I chid her for bringing evil days upon us by talking to the sacred cats of the priests, and carrying them in her arms. I told her she would be left alone here when the Romans came as a punishment for her disobedience. And now she is gone— run away—hidden. I speak the truth. I call Osiris to witness—

THE WOMEN [*protesting officiously*] She speaks the truth, Belzanor.

BELZANOR. You have frightened the child: she is hiding. Search—quick—into the palace—search every corner.

The guards, led by Belzanor, shoulder their way into the

palace through the flying crowd of women, who escape through the courtyard gate.

FTATATEETA [*screaming*] Sacrilege! Men in the Queen's chambers! Sa— [*her voice dies away as the Persian puts his knife to her throat*].

BEL AFFRIS [*laying a hand on Ftatateeta's left shoulder*] Forbear her yet a moment, Persian. [*To Ftatateeta, very significantly*] Mother: your gods are asleep or away hunting; and the sword is at your throat. Bring us to where the Queen is hid, and you shall live.

FTATATEETA [*contemptuously*] Who shall stay the sword in the hand of a fool, if the high gods put it there? Listen to me, ye young men without understanding. Cleopatra fears me; but she fears the Romans more. There is but one power greater in her eyes than the wrath of the Queen's nurse and the cruelty of Cæsar; and that is the power of the Sphinx that sits in the desert watching the way to the sea. What she would have it know, she tells into the ears of the sacred cats; and on her birthday she sacrifices to it and decks it with poppies. Go ye therefore into the desert and seek Cleopatra in the shadow of the Sphinx; and on your heads see to it that no harm comes to her.

BEL AFFRIS [*to the Persian*] May we believe this, O subtle one?

PERSIAN. Which way come the Romans?

BEL AFFRIS. Over the desert, from the sea, by this very Sphinx.

PERSIAN [*to Ftatateeta*] O mother of guile! O aspic's tongue! You have made up this tale so that we two may go into the desert and perish on the spears of the Romans. [*Lifting his knife*] Taste death.

FTATATEETA. Not from thee, baby. [*She snatches his ankle from under him and flies stooping along the palace wall, vanishing in the darkness within its precinct. Bel Affris roars with laughter as the Persian tumbles. The guardsmen rush out of the palace with Belzanor and a mob of fugitives, mostly carrying bundles*].

PERSIAN. Have you found Cleopatra?

BELZANOR. She is gone. We have searched every corner.

THE NUBIAN SENTINEL [*appearing at the door of the palace*] Woe! Alas! Fly, fly!

BELZANOR. What is the matter now?

THE NUBIAN SENTINEL. The sacred white cat has been stolen.

ALL. Woe! woe! [*General panic. They all fly with cries of consternation. The torch is thrown down and extinguished in the rush. The noise of the fugitives dies away. Darkness and dead silence*].

ACT I

The same darkness into which the temple of Ra and the Syrian palace vanished. The same silence. Suspense. Then the blackness and stillness break softly into silver mist and strange airs as the windswept harp of Memnon plays at the dawning of the moon. It rises full over the desert; and a vast horizon comes into relief, broken by a huge shape which soon reveals itself in the spreading radiance as a Sphinx pedestalled on the sands. The light still clears, until the up-raised eyes of the image are distinguished looking straight forward and upward in infinite fearless vigil, and a mass of color between its great paws defines itself as a heap of red poppies on which a girl lies motionless, her silken vest heaving gently and regularly with the breathing of a dreamless sleeper, and her braided hair glittering in a shaft of moonlight like a bird's wing.

Suddenly there comes from afar a vaguely fearful sound (it might be the bellow of a Minotaur softened by great distance) and Memnon's music stops. Silence: then a few faint high-ringing trumpet notes. Then silence again. Then a man comes from the south with stealing steps, ravished by the mystery of the night, all wonder, and halts, lost in contemplation, opposite the left flank of the Sphinx, whose bosom, with its burden, is hidden from him by its massive shoulder.

THE MAN. Hail, Sphinx: salutation from Julius Cæsar! I have wandered in many lands, seeking the lost regions from which my birth into this world exiled me, and the company of creatures such as I myself. I have found flocks and pastures, men and cities, but no other Cæsar, no air native to me, no man kindred to me, none who can do my day's deed, and think my night's thought. In the little world yonder, Sphinx, my place is as high as yours in this great desert; only I wander, and you sit still; I conquer, and you endure; I work and wonder, you watch and wait; I look up and am dazzled, look down and am darkened, look round and am puzzled, whilst your eyes never turn from looking out—out of the world—to the lost region—the home from which we have strayed. Sphinx, you and I, strangers to the race of men, are no strangers to one another: have I not been conscious of you and of this place since I was born? Rome is a madman's dream: this is my Reality. These starry lamps of yours I have seen from afar in Gaul, in Britain, in Spain, in Thessaly, signalling great secrets to some eternal sentinel below, whose post I never could find. And here at last is their sentinel—an image of the constant and immortal part of my life, silent, full of thoughts, alone in the silver desert. Sphinx, Sphinx: I have climbed mountains at night to hear in the distance the stealthy footfall of the winds that chase your sands in forbidden play—our invisible children, O Sphinx, laughing in whispers. My way hither was the way of destiny; for I am he of whose genius you are the symbol: part brute, part woman, and part god—nothing of man in me at all. Have I read your riddle, Sphinx?

THE GIRL [*who has wakened, and peeped cautiously from her nest to see who is speaking*] Old gentleman.

CÆSAR [*starting violently, and clutching his sword*] Immortal gods!

THE GIRL. Old gentleman: dont run away.

CÆSAR [*stupefied*] "Old gentleman: dont run away"!!! This! to Julius Cæsar!

THE GIRL [*urgently*] Old gentleman.

CÆSAR. Sphinx: you presume on your centuries. I am younger than you, though your voice is but a girl's voice as yet.

THE GIRL. Climb up here, quickly; or the Romans will come and eat you.

CÆSAR [*running forward past the Sphinx's shoulder, and seeing her*] A child at its breast! a divine child!

THE GIRL. Come up quickly. You must get up at its side and creep round.

CÆSAR [*amazed*] Who are you?

THE GIRL. Cleopatra, Queen of Egypt.

CÆSAR. Queen of the Gypsies, you mean.

CLEOPATRA. You must not be disrespectful to me, or the Sphinx will let the Romans eat you. Come up. It is quite cosy here.

CÆSAR [*to himself*] What a dream! What a magnificent dream! Only let me not wake, and I will conquer ten continents to pay for dreaming it out to the end. [*He climbs to the Sphinx's flank, and presently reappears to her on the pedestal, stepping round to its right shoulder*].

CLEOPATRA. Take care. Thats right. Now sit down: you may have its other paw. [*She seats herself comfortably on its left paw*]. It is very powerful and will protect us; but [*shivering, and with plaintive loneliness*] it would not take any notice of me or keep me company. I am glad you have come: I was very lonely. Did you happen to see a white cat anywhere?

CÆSAR [*sitting slowly down on the right paw in extreme wonderment*] Have you lost one?

CLEOPATRA. Yes: the sacred white cat: is it not dreadful? I brought him here to sacrifice him to the Sphinx; but when we got a little way from the city a black cat called him, and he jumped out of my arms and ran away to it. Do you think that the black cat can have been my great-great-great-grand-mother?

CÆSAR [*staring at her*] Your great-great-great-grand-mother! Well, why not? Nothing would surprise me on this night of nights.

CLEOPATRA. I think it must have been. My great-grand-mother's great-grandmother was a black kitten of the sacred white cat; and the river Nile made her his seventh wife.

That is why my hair is so wavy. And I always want to be let do as I like, no matter whether it is the will of the gods or not: that is because my blood is made with Nile water.

CÆSAR. What are you doing here at this time of night? Do you live here?

CLEOPATRA. Of course not: I am the Queen; and I shall live in the palace at Alexandria when I have killed my brother, who drove me out of it. When I am old enough I shall do just what I like. I shall be able to poison the slaves and see them wriggle, and pretend to Ftatateeta that she is going to be put into the fiery furnace.

CÆSAR. Hm! Meanwhile why are you not at home and in bed?

CLEOPATRA. Because the Romans are coming to eat us all. You are not at home and in bed either.

CÆSAR [with conviction] Yes I am. I live in a tent; and I am now in that tent, fast asleep and dreaming. Do you suppose that I believe you are real, you impossible little dream witch?

CLEOPATRA [giggling and leaning trustfully towards him] You are a funny old gentleman. I like you.

CÆSAR. Ah, that spoils the dream. Why dont you dream that I am young?

CLEOPATRA. I wish you were; only I think I should be more afraid of you. I like men, especially young men with round strong arms; but I am afraid of them. You are old and rather thin and stringy; but you have a nice voice; and I like to have somebody to talk to, though I think you are a little mad. It is the moon that makes you talk to yourself in that silly way.

CÆSAR. What! you heard that, did you? I was saying my prayers to the great Sphinx.

CLEOPATRA. But this isnt the great Sphinx.

CÆSAR [much disappointed, looking up at the statue] What!

CLEOPATRA. This is only a dear little kitten of a Sphinx.

Why, the great Sphinx is so big that it has a temple between its paws. This is my pet Sphinx. Tell me: do you think the Romans have any sorcerers who could take us away from the Sphinx by magic?

CÆSAR. Why? Are you afraid of the Romans?

CLEOPATRA [*very seriously*] Oh, they would eat us if they caught us. They are barbarians. Their chief is called Julius Cæsar. His father was a tiger and his mother a burning mountain; and his nose is like an elephant's trunk. [*Cæsar involuntarily rubs his nose*]. They all have long noses, and ivory tusks, and little tails, and seven arms with a hundred arrows in each; and they live on human flesh.

CÆSAR. Would you like me to shew you a real Roman?

CLEOPATRA [*terrified*] No. You are frightening me.

CÆSAR. No matter: this is only a dream—

CLEOPATRA [*excitedly*] It is not a dream: it is not a dream. See, see. [*She plucks a pin from her hair and jabs it repeatedly into his arm*].

CÆSAR. Ffff—Stop. [*Wrathfully*] How dare you?

CLEOPATRA [*abashed*] You said you were dreaming. [*Whimpering*] I only wanted to shew you—

CÆSAR [*gently*] Come, come: dont cry. A queen mustnt cry. [*He rubs his arm, wondering at the reality of the smart*]. Am I awake? [*He strikes his hand against the Sphinx to test its solidity. It feels so real that he begins to be alarmed, and says perplexedly*] Yes, I— [*quite panicstricken*] no: impossible: madness, madness! [*Desperately*] Back to camp—to camp. [*He rises to spring down from the pedestal*].

CLEOPATRA [*flinging her arms in terror round him*] No: you shant leave me. No, no, no: dont go. I'm afraid—afraid of the Romans.

CÆSAR [*as the conviction that he is really awake forces itself on him*] Cleopatra: can you see my face well?

CLEOPATRA. Yes. It is so white in the moonlight.

CÆSAR. Are you sure it is the moonlight that makes me look whiter than an Egyptian? [*Grimly*] Do you notice that

I have a rather long nose?

CLEOPATRA [*recoiling, paralysed by a terrible suspicion*] Oh!

CÆSAR. It is a Roman nose, Cleopatra.

CLEOPATRA. Ah! [*With a piercing scream she springs up; darts round the left shoulder of the Sphinx; scrambles down to the sand; and falls on her knees in frantic supplication, shrieking*] Bite him in two, Sphinx: bite him in two. I meant to sacrifice the white cat—I did indeed—I [*Cæsar, who has slipped down from the pedestal, touches her on the shoulder*]—Ah! [*She buries her head in her arms*].

CÆSAR. Cleopatra: shall I teach you a way to prevent Cæsar from eating you?

CLEOPATRA [*clinging to him piteously*] Oh do, do, do. I will steal Ftatateeta's jewels and give them to you. I will make the river Nile water your lands twice a year.

CÆSAR. Peace, peace, my child. Your gods are afraid of the Romans: you see the Sphinx dare not bite me, nor prevent me carrying you off to Julius Cæsar.

CLEOPATRA [*in pleading murmurings*] You wont, you wont. You said you wouldnt.

CÆSAR. Cæsar never eats women.

CLEOPATRA [*springing up full of hope*] What!

CÆSAR [*impressively*] But he eats girls [*she relapses*] and cats. Now you are a silly little girl; and you are descended from the black kitten. You are both a girl and a cat.

CLEOPATRA [*trembling*] And will he eat me?

CÆSAR. Yes; unless you make him believe that you are a woman.

CLEOPATRA. Oh, you must get a sorcerer to make a woman of me. Are you a sorcerer?

CÆSAR. Perhaps. But it will take a long time; and this very night you must stand face to face with Cæsar in the palace of your fathers.

CLEOPATRA. No, no. I darent.

CÆSAR. Whatever dread may be in your soul—however

terrible Cæsar may be to you—you must confront him as a brave woman and a great queen; and you must feel no fear. If your hand shakes: if you voice quavers; then—night and death! [*She moans*]. But if he thinks you worthy to rule, he will set you on the throne by his side and make you the real ruler of Egypt.

CLEOPATRA [*despairingly*] No: he will find me out: he will find me out.

CÆSAR [*rather mournfully*] He is easily deceived by women. Their eyes dazzle him; and he sees them not as they are, but as he wishes them to appear to him.

CLEOPATRA [*hopefully*] Then we will cheat him. I will put on Ftatateeta's head-dress; and he will think me quite an old woman.

CÆSAR. If you do that he will eat you at one mouthful.

CLEOPATRA. But I will give him a cake with my magic opal and seven hairs of the white cat baked in it; and—

CÆSAR [*abruptly*] Pah! you are a little fool. He will eat your cake and you too. [*He turns contemptuously from her*].

CLEOPATRA [*running after him and clinging to him*] Oh please, please! I will do whatever you tell me. I will be good. I will be your slave. [*Again the terrible bellowing note sounds across the desert, now closer at hand. It is the bucina, the Roman war trumpet*].

CÆSAR. Hark!

CLEOPATRA [*trembling*] What was that?

CÆSAR. Cæsar's voice.

CLEOPATRA [*pulling at his hand*] Let us run away. Come. Oh, come.

CÆSAR. You are safe with me until you stand on your throne to receive Cæsar. Now lead me thither.

CLEOPATRA [*only too glad to get away*] I will, I will. [*Again the bucina*]. Oh come, come, come: the gods are angry. Do you feel the earth shaking?

CÆSAR. It is the tread of Cæsar's legions.

CLEOPATRA [*drawing him away*] This way, quickly. And

let us look for the white cat as we go. It is he that has turned
you into a Roman.

CÆSAR. Incorrigible, oh, incorrigible! Away! [*He follows
her, the bucina sounding louder as they steal across the
desert. The moonlight wanes: the horizon again shews black
against the sky, broken only by the fantastic silhouette of the
Sphinx. The sky itself vanishes in darkness, from which
there is no relief until the gleam of a distant torch falls on
great Egyptian pillars supporting the roof of a majestic corridor. At the further end of this corridor a Nubian slave
appears carrying the torch. Cæsar, still led by Cleopatra,
follows him. They come down the corridor, Cæsar, peering
keenly about at the strange architecture, and at the pillar
shadows between which, as the passing torch makes them
hurry noiselessly backwards, figures of men with wings and
hawk's heads, and vast black marble cats, seem to flit in and
out of ambush. Further along, the wall turns a corner and
makes a spacious transept in which Cæsar sees, on his right,
a throne, and behind the throne a door. On each side of the
throne is a slender pillar with a lamp on it*].

CÆSAR. What place is this?

CLEOPATRA. This is where I sit on the throne when I am
allowed to wear my crown and robes. [*The slave holds his
torch to shew the throne*].

CÆSAR. Order the slave to light the lamps.

CLEOPATRA [*shyly*] Do you think I may?

CÆSAR. Of course. You are the Queen. [*She hesitates*]. Go
on.

CLEOPATRA [*timidly, to the slave*] Light all the lamps.

FTATATEETA [*suddenly coming from behind the throne*]
Stop. [*The slave stops. She turns sternly to Cleopatra, who
quails like a naughty child*]. Who is this you have with you;
and how dare you order the lamps to be lighted without my
permission? [*Cleopatra is dumb with apprehension*].

CÆSAR. Who is she?

CLEOPATRA. Ftatateeta.

FTATATEETA [*arrogantly*] Chief nurse to—

CÆSAR [*cutting her short*] I speak to the Queen. Be silent. [*To Cleopatra*] Is this how your servants know their places? Send her away; and do you [*to the slave*] do as the Queen has bidden. [*The slave lights the lamps. Meanwhile Cleopatra stands hesitating, afraid of Ftatateeta*]. You are the Queen: send her away.

CLEOPATRA [*cajoling*] Ftatateeta, dear: you must go away —just for a little.

CÆSAR. You are not commanding her to go away: you are begging her. You are no Queen. You will be eaten. Farewell. [*He turns to go*].

CLEOPATRA [*clutching him*] No, no, no. Dont leave me.

CÆSAR. A Roman does not stay with queens who are afraid of their slaves.

CLEOPATRA. I am not afraid. Indeed I am not afraid.

FTATATEETA. We shall see who is afraid here. [*Menacingly*] Cleopatra—

CÆSAR. On your knees, woman: am I also a child that you dare trifle with me? [*He points to the floor at Cleopatra's feet. Ftatateeta, half cowed, half savage, hesitates. Cæsar calls to the Nubian*] Slave. [*The Nubian comes to him*] Can you cut off a head? [*The Nubian nods and grins ecstatically, showing all his teeth. Cæsar takes his sword by the scabbard, ready to offer the hilt to the Nubian, and turns again to Ftatateeta, repeating his gesture*]. Have you remembered yourself, mistress?

Ftatateeta, crushed, kneels before Cleopatra, who can hardly believe her eyes.

FTATATEETA [*hoarsely*] O Queen, forget not thy servant in the days of thy greatness.

CLEOPATRA [*blazing with excitement*] Go. Begone. Go away. [*Ftatateeta rises with stooped head, and moves backwards towards the door. Cleopatra watches her submission eagerly, almost clapping her hands, which are trembling. Suddenly she cries*] Give me something to beat her with.

[*She snatches a snake-skin from the throne and dashes after Ftatateeta, whirling it like a scourge in the air. Cæsar makes a bound and manages to catch her and hold her while Ftatateeta escapes*].

CÆSAR. You scratch, kitten, do you?

CLEOPATRA [*breaking from him*] I will beat somebody. I will beat him. [*She attacks the slave*]. There, there, there! [*The slave flies for his life up the corridor and vanishes. She throws the snake-skin away and jumps on the step of the throne with her arms waving, crying*] I am a real Queen at last—a real, real Queen! Cleopatra the Queen! [*Cæsar shakes his head dubiously, the advantage of the change seeming open to question from the point of view of the general welfare of Egypt. She turns and looks at him exultantly. Then she jumps down from the steps, runs to him, and flings her arms round him rapturously, crying*] Oh, I love you for making me a Queen.

CÆSAR. But queens love only kings.

CLEOPATRA. I will make all the men I love kings. I will make you a king. I will have many young kings, with round, strong arms; and when I am tired of them I will whip them to death; but you shall always be my king: my nice, kind, wise, good old king.

CÆSAR. Oh, my wrinkles, my wrinkles! And my child's heart! You will be the most dangerous of all Cæsar's conquests.

CLEOPATRA [*appalled*] Cæsar! I forgot Cæsar. [*Anxiously*] You will tell him that I am a Queen, will you not?—a real Queen. Listen! [*stealthily coaxing him*]: let us run away and hide until Cæsar is gone.

CÆSAR. If you fear Cæsar, you are no true queen; and though you were to hide beneath a pyramid, he would go straight to it and lift it with one hand. And then—! [*he chops his teeth together*].

CLEOPATRA [*trembling*] Oh!

CÆSAR. Be afraid if you dare. [*The note of the bucina*

*resounds again in the distance. She moans with fear. Cæsar
exults in it, exclaiming*] Aha! Cæsar approaches the throne of
Cleopatra. Come: take your place. [*He takes her hand and
leads her to the throne. She is too downcast to speak*]. Ho,
there, Teetatota. How do you call your slaves?

CLEOPATRA [*spiritlessly, as she sinks on the throne and
cowers there, shaking*] Clap your hands.

He claps his hands. Ftatateeta returns.

CÆSAR. Bring the Queen's robes, and her crown, and her
women; and prepare her.

CLEOPATRA [*eagerly—recovering herself a little*] Yes, the
crown, Ftatateeta: I shall wear the crown.

FTATATEETA. For whom must the Queen put on her state?

CÆSAR. For a citizen of Rome. A king of kings, Totateeta.

CLEOPATRA [*stamping at her*] How dare you ask questions?
Go and do as you are told. [*Ftatateeta goes out with a grim
smile. Cleopatra goes on eagerly, to Cæsar*] Cæsar will know
that I am a Queen when he sees my crown and robes, will
he not?

CÆSAR. No. How shall he know that you are not a slave
dressed up in the Queen's ornaments?

CLEOPATRA. You must tell him.

CÆSAR. He will not ask me. He will know Cleopatra by her
pride, her courage, her majesty, and her beauty. [*She looks
very doubtful*] Are you trembling?

CLEOPATRA [*shivering with dread*] No, I—I— [*in a very
sickly voice*] No.

Ftatateeta and three women come in with the regalia.

FTATATEETA. Of all the Queen's women, these three alone
are left. The rest are fled. [*They begin to deck Cleopatra,
who submits, pale and motionless*].

CÆSAR. Good, good. Three are enough. Poor Cæsar generally has to dress himself.

FTATATEETA [*contemptuously*] The queen of Egypt is not
a Roman barbarian. [*To Cleopatra*] Be brave, my nursling.
Hold up your head before this stranger.

CÆSAR [*admiring Cleopatra, and placing the crown on her head*] Is it sweet or bitter to be a Queen, Cleopatra?

CLEOPATRA. Bitter.

CÆSAR. Cast out fear; and you will conquer Cæsar. Tota: are the Romans at hand?

FTATATEETA. They are at hand; and the guard has fled.

THE WOMEN [*wailing subduedly*] Woe to us!

The Nubian comes running down the hall.

NUBIAN. The Romans are in the courtyard. [*He bolts through the door. With a shriek, the women fly after him. Ftatateeta's jaw expresses savage resolution: she does not budge. Cleopatra can hardly restrain herself from following them. Cæsar grips her wrist, and looks steadfastly at her. She stands like a martyr*].

CÆSAR. The Queen must face Cæsar alone. Answer "So be it."

CLEOPATRA [*white*] So be it.

CÆSAR [*releasing her*] Good.

A tramp and tumult of armed men is heard. Cleopatra's terror increases. The bucina sounds close at hand, followed by a formidable clangor of trumpets. This is too much for Cleopatra: she utters a cry and darts towards the door. Ftatateeta stops her ruthlessly.

FTATATEETA. You are my nursling. You have said "So be it"; and if you die for it, you must make the Queen's word good. [*She hands Cleopatra to Cæsar, who takes her back, almost beside herself with apprehension, to the throne*].

CÆSAR. Now, if you quail—! [*He seats himself on the throne*].

She stands on the step, all but unconscious, waiting for death. The Roman soldiers troop in tumultuously through the corridor, headed by their ensign with his eagle, and their bucinator, a burly fellow with his instrument coiled round his body, its brazen bell shaped like the head of a howling wolf. When they reach the transept, they stare in amazement at the throne; dress into ordered rank opposite; draw their swords and lift them in the air with a shout of Hail, Cæsar. *Cleopatra turns and stares wildly at Cæsar; grasps the situation; and, with a great sob of relief, falls into his arms.*

ACT II

Alexandria. A hall on the first floor of the Palace, ending in a loggia approached by two steps. Through the arches of the loggia the Mediterranean can be seen, bright in the morning sun. The clean lofty walls, painted with a procession of the Egyptian theocracy, presented in profile as flat ornament, and the absence of mirrors, sham perspectives, stuffy upholstery and textiles, make the place handsome, wholesome, simple and cool, or, as a rich English manufacturer would express it, poor, bare, ridiculous and unhomely. For Tottenham Court Road civilization is to this Egyptian civilization as glass bead and tattoo civilization is to Tottenham Court Road.

The young king Ptolemy Dionysus (aged ten) is at the top of the steps, on his way in through the loggia, led by his guardian Pothinus, who has him by the hand. The court is assembled to receive him. It is made up of men and women (some of the women being officials) of various complexions and races, mostly Egyptian; some of them, comparatively fair, from lower Egypt, some, much darker, from upper Egypt; with a few Greeks and Jews. Prominent in a group on Ptolemy's right hand is Theodotus, Ptolemy's tutor. Another group, on Ptolemy's left, is headed by Achillas, the general of Ptolemy's troops. Theodotus is a little old man, whose features are as cramped and wizened as his limbs, except his tall straight forehead, which occupies more space than all the rest of his face. He maintains an air of magpie keenness and profundity, listening to what the others says with the sarcastic vigilance of a philosopher listening to the exercises of his disciples. Achillas is a tall handsome man of thirty-five, with a fine black beard curled like the coat of a poodle. Apparently not a clever man, but distinguished and dignified. Pothinus is a vigorous man of fifty, a eunuch, passionate,

energetic and quick witted, but of common mind and charac-
ter; impatient and unable to control his temper. He has fine
tawny hair, like fur. Ptolemy, the King, looks much older
than an English boy of ten; but he has the childish air, the
habit of being in leading strings, the mixture of impotence
and petulance, the appearance of being excessively washed,
combed and dressed by other hands, which is exhibited by
court-bred princes of all ages.

All receive the King with reverences. He comes down the
steps to a chair of state which stands a little to his right, the
only seat in the hall. Taking his place before it, he looks
nervously for instructions to Pothinus, who places himself at
his left hand.

POTHINUS. The king of Egypt has a word to speak.

THEODOTUS [*in a squeak which he makes impressive by*
sheer self-opinionativeness] Peace for the King's word!

PTOLEMY [*without any vocal inflexions: he is evidently re-*
peating a lesson] Take notice of this all of you. I am the
first-born son of Auletes the Flute Blower who was your
King. My sister Berenice drove him from his throne and
reigned in his stead but—but— [*he hesitates*]—

POTHINUS [*stealthily prompting*]—but the gods would not
suffer—

PTOLEMY. Yes—the gods would not suffer—not suffer—
[*He stops; then, crestfallen*] I forgot what the gods would
not suffer.

THEODOTUS. Let Pothinus, the King's guardian, speak for
the King.

POTHINUS [*suppressing his impatience with difficulty*] The
King wished to say that the gods would not suffer the im-
piety of his sister to go unpunished.

PTOLEMY [*hastily*] Yes: I remember the rest of it. [*He*
resumes his monotone]. Therefore the gods sent a stranger
one Mark Antony a Roman captain of horsemen across the
sands of the desert and he set my father again upon the

throne. And my father took Berenice my sister and struck her head off. And now that my father is dead yet another of his daughters my sister Cleopatra would snatch the kingdom from me and reign in my place. But the gods would not suffer— [*Pothinus coughs admonitorily*]—the gods—the gods would not suffer—

POTHINUS [*prompting*]—will not maintain—

PTOLEMY. Oh yes—will not maintain such iniquity they will give her head to the axe even as her sister's. But with the help of the witch Ftatateeta she hath cast a spell on the Roman Julius Cæsar to make him uphold her false pretence to rule in Egypt. Take notice then that I will not suffer— that I will not suffer—[*pettishly, to Pothinus*] What is it that I will not suffer?

POTHINUS [*suddenly exploding with all the force and emphasis of political passion*] The King will not suffer a foreigner to take from him the throne of our Egypt. [*A shout of applause*]. Tell the King, Achillas, how many soldiers and horsemen follow the Roman?

THEODOTUS. Let the King's general speak!

ACHILLAS. But two Roman legions, O King. Three thousand soldiers and scarce a thousand horsemen.

The court breaks into derisive laughter; and a great chattering begins, amid which Rufio, a Roman officer, appears in the loggia. He is a burly, black-bearded man of middle age, very blunt, prompt and rough, with small clear eyes, and plump nose and cheeks, which, however, like the rest of his flesh, are in ironhard condition.

RUFIO [*from the steps*] Peace, ho! [*The laughter and chatter cease abruptly*]. Cæsar approaches.

THEODOTUS [*with much presence of mind*] The King permits the Roman commander to enter!

Cæsar, plainly dressed, but wearing an oak wreath to conceal his baldness, enters from the loggia, attended by Britannus, his secretary, a Briton, about forty, tall, solemn, and already slightly bald, with a heavy, drooping, hazel-colored moustache trained so as to lose its ends in a pair of trim whiskers. He is carefully dressed in blue, with portfolio, inkhorn, and reed pen at his girdle. His serious air and sense of the importance of the business in hand is in marked contrast to the kindly interest of Cæsar, who looks at the scene, which is new to him, with the frank curiosity of a child, and then turns to the king's chair: Britannus and Rufio posting themselves near the steps at the other side.

CÆSAR [*looking at Pothinus and Ptolemy*] Which is the King? the man or the boy?

POTHINUS. I am Pothinus, the guardian of my lord the King.

CÆSAR [*patting Ptolemy kindly on the shoulder*] So you are the King. Dull work at your age, eh? [*To Pothinus*] Your servant, Pothinus. [*He turns away unconcernedly and comes slowly along the middle of the hall, looking from side to side at the courtiers until he reaches Achillas*]. And this gentleman?

THEODOTUS. Achillas, the King's general.

CÆSAR [*to Achillas, very friendly*] A general, eh? I am a general myself. But I began too old, too old. Health and many victories, Achillas!

ACHILLAS. As the gods will, Cæsar.

CÆSAR [*turning to Theodotus*] And you, sir, are—?

THEODOTUS. Theodotus, the King's tutor.

CÆSAR. You teach men how to be kings, Theodotus. That is very clever of you. [*Looking at the gods on the walls as he turns away from Theodotus and goes up again to Pothinus*] And this place?

POTHINUS. The council chamber of the chancellors of the King's treasury, Cæsar.

CÆSAR. Ah! that reminds me. I want some money.

POTHINUS. The King's treasury is poor, Cæsar.

CÆSAR. Yes: I notice that there is but one chair in it.

RUFIO [*shouting gruffly*] Bring a chair there, some of you, for Cæsar.

PTOLEMY [*rising shyly to offer his chair*] Cæsar—

CÆSAR [*kindly*] No, no, my boy: that is your chair of state. Sit down.

He makes Ptolemy sit down again. Meanwhile Rufio, looking about him, sees in the nearest corner an image of the god Ra, represented as a seated man with the head of a hawk. Before the image is a bronze tripod, about as large as a three-legged stool, with a stick of incense burning on it. Rufio, with Roman resourcefulness and indifference to foreign superstitions, promptly seizes the tripod; shakes off the incense; blows away the ash; and dumps it down behind Cæsar, nearly in the middle of the hall.

RUFIO. Sit on that, Cæsar.

A shiver runs through the court, followed by a hissing whisper of Sacrilege!

CÆSAR [*seating himself*] Now, Pothinus, to business. I am badly in want of money.

BRITANNUS [*disapproving of these informal expressions*] My master would say that there is a lawful debt due to Rome by Egypt, contracted by the King's deceased father to the Triumvirate; and that it is Cæsar's duty to his country to require immediate payment.

CÆSAR [*blandly*] Ah, I forgot. I have not made my companions known here. Pothinus: this is Britannus, my secretary. He is an islander from the western end of the world, a day's voyage from Gaul. [*Britannus bows stiffly*]. This gentleman is Rufio, my comrade in arms. [*Rufio nods*]. Pothinus: I want 1,600 talents.

The courtiers, appalled, murmur loudly, and Theodotus and Achillas appeal mutely to one another against so monstrous a demand.

POTHINUS [*aghast*] Forty million sesterces! Impossible. There is not so much money in the King's treasury.

CÆSAR [*encouragingly*] Only sixteen hundred talents, Pothinus. Why count it in sesterces? A sestertius is only worth a loaf of bread.

POTHINUS. And a talent is worth a racehorse. I say it is impossible. We have been at strife here, because the King's sister Cleopatra falsely claims his throne. The King's taxes have not been collected for a whole year.

CÆSAR. Yes they have, Pothinus. My officers have been collecting them all morning. [Renewed whisper and sensation, not without some stifled laughter, among the courtiers].

RUFIO [bluntly] You must pay, Pothinus. Why waste words? You are getting off cheaply enough.

POTHINUS [bitterly] Is it possible that Cæsar, the conqueror of the world, has time to occupy himself with such a trifle as our taxes?

CÆSAR. My friend: taxes are the chief business of a conqueror of the world.

POTHINUS. Then take warning, Cæsar. This day, the treasures of the temple and the gold of the King's treasury shall be sent to the mint to be melted down for our ransom in the sight of the people. They shall see us sitting under bare walls and drinking from wooden cups. And their wrath be on your head, Cæsar, if you force us to this sacrilege!

CÆSAR. Do not fear, Pothinus: the people know how well wine tastes in wooden cups. In return for your bounty, I will settle this dispute about the throne for you, if you will. What say you?

POTHINUS. If I say no, will that hinder you?

RUFIO [defiantly] No.

CÆSAR. You say the matter has been at issue for a year, Pothinus. May I have ten minutes at it?

POTHINUS. You will do your pleasure, doubtless.

CÆSAR. Good! But first, let us have Cleopatra here.

THEODOTUS. She is not in Alexandria: she is fled into Syria.

CÆSAR. I think not. [To Rufio] Call Totateeta.

RUFIO [calling] Ho there, Teetatota.

Ftatateeta enters the loggia, and stands arrogantly at the top of the steps.

FTATATEETA. Who pronounces the name of Ftatateeta, the

Queen's chief nurse?

CÆSAR. Nobody can pronounce it, Tota, except yourself. Where is your mistress?

Cleopatra, who is hiding behind Ftatateeta, peeps out at them, laughing. Cæsar rises.

CÆSAR. Will the Queen favor us with her presence for a moment?

CLEOPATRA [*pushing Ftatateeta aside and standing haughtily on the brink of the steps*] Am I to behave like a Queen?

CÆSAR. Yes.

Cleopatra immediately comes down to the chair of state; seizes Ptolemy; drags him out of his seat; then takes his place in the chair. Ftatateeta seats herself on the step of the loggia, and sits there, watching the scene with sibylline intensity.

PTOLEMY [*mortified, and struggling with his tears*] Cæsar: this is how she treats me always. If I am king why is she allowed to take everything from me?

CLEOPATRA. You are not to be King, you little cry-baby. You are to be eaten by the Romans.

CÆSAR [*touched by Ptolemy's distress*] Come here, my boy, and stand by me.

Ptolemy goes over to Cæsar, who, resuming his seat on the tripod, takes the boy's hand to encourage him. Cleopatra, furiously jealous, rises and glares at them.

CLEOPATRA [*with flaming cheeks*] Take your throne: I dont want it. [*She flings away from the chair, and approaches Ptolemy, who shrinks from her*]. Go this instant and sit down in your place.

CÆSAR. Go, Ptolemy. Always take a throne when it is offered to you.

RUFIO. I hope you will have the good sense to follow your own advice when we return to Rome, Cæsar.

Ptolemy slowly goes back to the throne, giving Cleopatra a wide berth, in evident fear of her hands. She takes his place beside Cæsar.

CÆSAR. Pothinus—

CLEOPATRA [*interrupting him*] Are you not going to speak to me?

CÆSAR. Be quiet. Open your mouth again before I give you leave; and you shall be eaten.

CLEOPATRA. I am not afraid. A queen must not be afraid. Eat my husband there, if you like: he is afraid.

CÆSAR [*starting*] Your husband! What do you mean?

CLEOPATRA [*pointing to Ptolemy*] That little thing.

The two Romans and the Briton stare at one another in amazement.

THEODOTUS. Cæsar: you are a stranger here, and not conversant with our laws. The kings and queens of Egypt may not marry except with their own royal blood. Ptolemy and Cleopatra are born king and consort just as they are born brother and sister.

BRITANNUS [*shocked*] Cæsar: this is not proper.

THEODOTUS [*outraged*] How!

CÆSAR [*recovering his self-possession*] Pardon him, Theodotus: he is a barbarian, and thinks that the customs of his tribe and island are the laws of nature.

BRITANNUS. On the contrary, Cæsar, it is these Egyptians who are barbarians; and you do wrong to encourage them. I say it is a scandal.

CÆSAR. Scandal or not, my friend, it opens the gate of peace. [*He addresses Pothinus seriously*]. Pothinus: hear what I propose.

RUFIO. Hear Cæsar there.

CÆSAR. Ptolemy and Cleopatra shall reign jointly in Egypt.

ACHILLAS. What of the King's younger brother and Cleopatra's younger sister?

RUFIO [*explaining*] There is another little Ptolemy, Cæsar: so they tell me.

CÆSAR. Well, the little Ptolemy can marry the other sister; and we will make them both a present of Cyprus.

POTHINUS [*impatiently*] Cyprus is of no use to anybody.

CÆSAR. No matter: you shall have it for the sake of peace.

BRITANNUS [*unconsciously anticipating a later statesman*] Peace with honor, Pothinus.

POTHINUS [*mutinously*] Cæsar: be honest. The money you demand is the price of our freedom. Take it; and leave us to settle our own affairs.

THE BOLDER COURTIERS [*encouraged by Pothinus's tone and Cæsar's quietness*] Yes, yes. Egypt for the Egyptians!

The conference now becomes an altercation, the Egyptians becoming more and more heated. Cæsar remains unruffled; but Rufio grows fiercer and doggeder, and Britannus haughtily indignant.

RUFIO [*contemptuously*] Egypt for the Egyptians! Do you forget that there is a Roman army of occupation here, left by Aulus Gabinius when he set up your toy king for you?

ACHILLAS [*suddenly asserting himself*] And now under my command. *I* am the Roman general here, Cæsar.

CÆSAR [*tickled by the humor of the situation*] And also the Egyptian general, eh?

POTHINUS [*triumphantly*] That is so, Cæsar.

CÆSAR [*to Achillas*] So you can make war on the Egyptians in the name of Rome, and on the Romans—on me, if necessary—in the name of Egypt?

ACHILLAS. That is so, Cæsar.

CÆSAR. And which side are you on at present, if I may presume to ask, general?

ACHILLAS. On the side of the right and of the gods.

CÆSAR. Hm! How many men have you?

ACHILLAS. That will appear when I take the field.

RUFIO [*truculently*] Are your men Romans? If not, it matters not how many there are, provided you are no stronger than 500 to ten.

POTHINUS. It is useless to try to bluff us, Rufio. Cæsar has been defeated before and may be defeated again. A few weeks ago Cæsar was flying for his life before Pompey: a few months hence he may be flying for his life before Cato and Juba of Numidia, the African King.

ACHILLAS [*following up Pothinus's speech menacingly*] What can you do with 4,000 men?

THEODOTUS [*following up Achillas's speech with a raucous squeak*] And without money? Away with you.

ALL THE COURTIERS [*shouting fiercely and crowding towards Cæsar*] Away with you. Egypt for the Egyptians! Begone.

Rufio bites his beard, too angry to speak. Cæsar sits as comfortably as if he were at breakfast, and the cat were clamoring for a piece of Finnan-haddie.

CLEOPATRA. Why do you let them talk to you like that, Cæsar? Are you afraid?

CÆSAR. Why, my dear, what they say is quite true.

CLEOPATRA. But if you go away, I shall not be Queen.

CÆSAR. I shall not go away until you are Queen.

POTHINUS. Achillas: if you are not a fool, you will take that girl whilst she is under your hand.

RUFIO [*daring them*] Why not take Cæsar as well, Achillas?

POTHINUS [*retorting the defiance with interest*] Well said, Rufio. Why not?

RUFIO. Try, Achillas. [*Calling*] Guard there.

The loggia immediately fills with Cæsar's soldiers, who stand, sword in hand, at the top of the steps, waiting the word to charge from their centurion, who carries a cudgel. For a moment the Egyptians face them proudly: then they retire sullenly to their former places.

BRITANNUS. You are Cæsar's prisoners, all of you.

CÆSAR [*benevolently*] Oh no, no, no. By no means. Cæsar's guests, gentlemen.

CLEOPATRA. Wont you cut their heads off?

CÆSAR. What! Cut off your brother's head?

CLEOPATRA. Why not? He would cut off mine, if he got the chance. Wouldnt you, Ptolemy?

PTOLEMY [*pale and obstinate*] I would. I will, too, when

I grow up.

*Cleopatra is rent by a struggle between her newly-acquired
dignity as a queen, and a strong impulse to put out her
tongue at him. She takes no part in the scene which follows,
but watches it with curiosity and wonder, fidgeting with the
restlessness of a child, and sitting down on Cæsar's tripod
when he rises.*

POTHINUS. Cæsar: if you attempt to detain us—

RUFIO. He will succeed, Egyptian: make up your mind to
that. We hold the palace, the beach, and the eastern harbor.
The road to Rome is open; and you shall travel it if Cæsar
chooses.

CÆSAR [*courteously*] I could do no less, Pothinus, to secure
the retreat of my own soldiers. I am accountable for every
life among them. But you are free to go. So are all here, and
in the palace.

RUFIO [*aghast at this clemency*] What! Renegades and all?

CÆSAR [*softening the expression*] Roman army of occupation and all, Rufio.

POTHINUS [*bewildered*] But—but—but—

CÆSAR. Well, my friend?

POTHINUS. You are turning us out of our own palace into
the streets; and you tell us with a grand air that we are free
to go! It is for you to go.

CÆSAR. Your friends are in the street, Pothinus. You will
be safer there.

POTHINUS. This is a trick. I am the king's guardian: I refuse
to stir. I stand on my right here. Where is your right?

CÆSAR. It is in Rufio's scabbard, Pothinus. I may not be able
to keep it there if you wait too long.

Sensation.

POTHINUS [*bitterly*] And this is Roman justice!

THEODOTUS. But not Roman gratitude, I hope.

CÆSAR. Gratitude! Am I in your debt for any service, gentlemen?

THEODOTUS. Is Cæsar's life of so little account to him that

he forgets that we have saved it?

CÆSAR. My life! Is that all?

THEODOTUS. Your life. Your laurels. Your future.

POTHINUS. It is true. I can call a witness to prove that but for us, the Roman army of occupation, led by the greatest soldier in the world, would now have Cæsar at its mercy. [*Calling through the loggia*] Ho, there, Lucius Septimius [*Cæsar starts, deeply moved*]: if my voice can reach you, come forth and testify before Cæsar.

CÆSAR [*shrinking*] No, no.

THEODOTUS. Yes, I say. Let the military tribune bear witness.

Lucius Septimius, a clean shaven, trim athlete of about 40, with symmetrical features, resolute mouth, and handsome, thin Roman nose, in the dress of a Roman officer, comes in through the loggia and confronts Cæsar, who hides his face with his robe for a moment; then, mastering himself, drops it, and confronts the tribune with dignity.

POTHINUS. Bear witness, Lucius Septimius. Cæsar came hither in pursuit of his foe. Did we shelter his foe?

LUCIUS. As Pompey's foot touched the Egyptian shore, his head fell by the stroke of my sword.

THEODOTUS [*with viperish relish*] Under the eyes of his wife and child! Remember that, Cæsar! They saw it from the ship he had just left. We have given you a full and sweet measure of vengeance.

CÆSAR [*with horror*] Vengeance!

POTHINUS. Our first gift to you, as your galley came into the roadstead, was the head of your rival for the empire of the world. Bear witness, Lucius Septimius: is it not so?

LUCIUS. It is so. With this hand, that slew Pompey, I placed his head at the feet of Cæsar.

CÆSAR. Murderer! So would you have slain Cæsar, had Pompey been victorious at Pharsalia.

LUCIUS. Woe to the vanquished, Cæsar! When I served Pompey, I slew as good men as he, only because he conquered them. His turn came at last.

THEODOTUS [*flatteringly*] The deed was not yours, Cæsar, but ours—nay, mine; for it was done by my counsel. Thanks to us, you keep your reputation for clemency, and have your vengeance too.

CÆSAR. Vengeance! Vengeance!! Oh, if I could stoop to vengeance, what would I not exact from you as the price of this murdered man's blood? [*They shrink back, appalled and disconcerted*]. Was he not my son-in-law, my ancient friend, for 20 years the master of great Rome, for 30 years the compeller of victory? Did not I, as a Roman, share his glory? Was the Fate that forced us to fight for the mastery of the world, of our making? Am I Julius Cæsar, or am I a wolf, that you fling to me the grey head of the old soldier, the laurelled conqueror, the mighty Roman, treacherously struck down by this callous ruffian, and then claim my gratitude for it! [*To Lucius Septimius*] Begone: you fill me with horror.

LUCIUS [*cold and undaunted*] Pshaw! You have seen severed heads before, Cæsar, and severed right hands too, I think; some thousands of them, in Gaul, after you vanquished Vercingetorix. Did you spare him, with all your clemency? Was that vengeance?

CÆSAR. No, by the gods! would that it had been! Vengeance at least is human. No, I say: those severed right hands, and the brave Vercingetorix basely strangled in a vault beneath the Capitol were [*with shuddering satire*] a wise severity, a necessary protection to the commonwealth, a duty of statesmanship—follies and fictions ten times bloodier than honest vengeance! What a fool was I then! To think that men's lives should be at the mercy of such fools! [*Humbly*] Lucius Septimius, pardon me: why should the slayer of Vercingetorix rebuke the slayer of Pompey? You are free to go with the rest. Or stay if you will: I will find a place for you in my service.

LUCIUS. The odds are against you, Cæsar. I go. [*He turns

to go out through the loggia].

RUFIO [*full of wrath at seeing his prey escaping*] That means that he is a Republican.

LUCIUS [*turning defiantly on the loggia steps*] And what are you?

RUFIO. A Cæsarian, like all Cæsar's soldiers.

CÆSAR [*courteously*] Lucius: believe me, Cæsar is no Cæsarian. Were Rome a true republic, then were Cæsar the first of Republicans. But you have made your choice. Farewell.

LUCIUS. Farewell. Come, Achillas, whilst there is yet time.

Cæsar, seeing that Rufio's temper threatens to get the worse of him, puts his hand on his shoulder and brings him down the hall out of harm's way, Britannus accompanying them and posting himself on Cæsar's right hand. This movement brings the three in a little group to the place occupied by Achillas, who moves haughtily away and joins Theodotus on the other side. Lucius Septimius goes out through the soldiers in the loggia. Pothinus, Theodotus and Achillas follow him with the courtiers, very mistrustful of the soldiers, who close up in their rear and go out after them, keeping them moving without much ceremony. The King is left in his chair, piteous, obstinate, with twitching face and fingers. During these movements Rufio maintains an energetic grumbling, as follows:—

RUFIO [*as Lucius departs*] Do you suppose he would let us go if he had our heads in his hands?

CÆSAR. I have no right to suppose that his ways are any baser than mine.

RUFIO. Psha!

CÆSAR. Rufio: if I take Lucius Septimius for my model, and become exactly like him, ceasing to be Cæsar, will you serve me still?

BRITANNUS. Cæsar: this is not good sense. Your duty to Rome demands that her enemies should be prevented from doing further mischief. [*Cæsar, whose delight in the moral eye-to-business of his British secretary is inexhaustible, smiles indulgently*].

RUFIO. It is no use talking to him, Britannus: you may save your breath to cool your porridge. But mark this, Cæsar. Clemency is very well for you; but what is it for your soldiers, who have to fight tomorrow the men you spared yesterday? You may give what orders you please; but I tell you that your next victory will be a massacre, thanks to your clemency. I, for one, will take no prisoners. I will kill my enemies in the field; and then you can preach as much clemency as you please: I shall never have to fight them again. And now, with your leave, I will see these gentry off the premises. [*He turns to go*].

CÆSAR [*turning also and seeing Ptolemy*] What! have they left the boy alone! Oh shame, shame!

RUFIO [*taking Ptolemy's hand and making him rise*] Come, your majesty!

PTOLEMY [*to Cæsar, drawing away his hand from Rufio*] Is he turning me out of my palace?

RUFIO [*grimly*] You are welcome to stay if you wish.

CÆSAR [*kindly*] Go, my boy. I will not harm you; but you will be safer away, among your friends. Here you are in the lion's mouth.

PTOLEMY [*turning to go*] It is not the lion I fear, but [*looking at Rufio*] the jackal. [*He goes out through the loggia*].

CÆSAR [*laughing approvingly*] Brave boy!

CLEOPATRA [*jealous of Cæsar's approbation, calling after Ptolemy*] Little silly. You think that very clever.

CÆSAR. Britannus: attend the King. Give him in charge to that Pothinus fellow. [*Britannus goes out after Ptolemy*].

RUFIO [*pointing to Cleopatra*] And this piece of goods? What is to be done with her? However, I suppose I may leave that to you. [*He goes out through the loggia*].

CLEOPATRA [*flushing suddenly and turning on Cæsar*] Did you mean me to go with the rest?

CÆSAR [*a little preoccupied, goes with a sigh to Ptolemy's chair, whilst she waits for his answer with red cheeks and clenched fists]* You are free to do just as you please, Cleopatra.

CLEOPATRA. Then you do not care whether I stay or not?

CÆSAR [*smiling*] Of course I had rather you stayed.

CLEOPATRA. Much, much rather?

CÆSAR [*nodding*] Much, much rather.

CLEOPATRA. Then I consent to stay, because I am asked. But I do not want to, mind.

CÆSAR. That is quite understood. [*Calling*] Totateeta.

Ftatateeta, still seated, turns her eyes on him with a sinister expression, but does not move.

CLEOPATRA [*with a splutter of laughter*] Her name is not Totateeta: it is Ftatateeta. [*Calling*] Ftatateeta. [*Ftatateeta instantly rises and comes to Cleopatra*].

CÆSAR [*stumbling over the name*] Tfatafeeta will forgive the erring tongue of a Roman. Tota: the Queen will hold her state here in Alexandria. Engage women to attend upon her; and do all that is needful.

FTATATEETA. Am I then the mistress of the Queen's household?

CLEOPATRA [*sharply*] No: *I* am the mistress of the Queen's household. Go and do as you are told, or I will have you thrown into the Nile this very afternoon, to poison the poor crocodiles.

CÆSAR [*shocked*] Oh no, no.

CLEOPATRA. Oh yes, yes. You are very sentimental, Cæsar; but you are clever; and if you do as I tell you, you will soon learn to govern.

Cæsar, quite dumbfounded by this impertinence, turns in his chair and stares at her.

Ftatateeta, smiling grimly, and shewing a splendid set of teeth, goes, leaving them alone together.

CÆSAR. Cleopatra: I really think I must eat you, after all.

CLEOPATRA [*kneeling beside him and looking at him with eager interest, half real, half affected to shew how intelligent she is*] You must not talk to me now as if I were a child.

CÆSAR. You have been growing up since the sphinx intro-
duced us the other night; and you think you know more
than I do already.

CLEOPATRA [*taken down, and anxious to justify herself*]
No: that would be very silly of me: of course I know that.
But—[*suddenly*] are you angry with me?

CÆSAR. No.

CLEOPATRA [*only half believing him*] Then why are you so
thoughtful?

CÆSAR [*rising*] I have work to do, Cleopatra.

CLEOPATRA [*drawing back*] Work! [*Offended*] You are
tired of talking to me; and that is your excuse to get away
from me.

CÆSAR [*sitting down again to appease her*] Well, well:
another minute. But then—work!

CLEOPATRA. Work! what nonsense! You must remember
that you are a king now: I have made you one. Kings dont
work.

CÆSAR. Oh! Who told you that, little kitten? Eh?

CLEOPATRA. My father was King of Egypt; and he never
worked. But he was a great king, and cut off my sister's head
because she rebelled against him and took the throne from
him.

CÆSAR. Well; and how did he get his throne back again?

CLEOPATRA [*eagerly, her eyes lighting up*] I will tell you.
A beautiful young man, with strong round arms, came over
the desert with many horsemen, and slew my sister's husband and gave my father back his throne. [*Wistfully*] I was
only twelve then. Oh, I wish he would come again, now that
I am queen. I would make him my husband.

CÆSAR. It might be managed, perhaps; for it was I who
sent that beautiful young man to help your father.

CLEOPATRA [*enraptured*] You know him!

CÆSAR [*nodding*] I do.

CLEOPATRA. Has he come with you? [*Cæsar shakes his*

head: she is cruelly disappointed]. Oh, I wish he had, I wish he had. If only I were a little older; so that he might not think me a mere kitten, as you do! But perhaps that is because you are old. He is many many years younger than you, is he not?

CÆSAR [*as if swallowing a pill*] He is somewhat younger.

CLEOPATRA. Would he be my husband, do you think, if I asked him?

CÆSAR. Very likely.

CLEOPATRA. But I should not like to ask him. Could you not persuade him to ask me—without knowing that I wanted him to?

CÆSAR [*touched by her innocence of the beautiful young man's character*] My poor child!

CLEOPATRA. Why do you say that as if you were sorry for me? Does he love anyone else?

CÆSAR. I am afraid so.

CLEOPATRA [*tearfully*] Then I shall not be his first love.

CÆSAR. Not quite the first. He is greatly admired by women.

CLEOPATRA. I wish I could be the first. But if he loves me, I will make him kill all the rest. Tell me: is he still beautiful? Do his strong round arms shine in the sun like marble?

CÆSAR. He is in excellent condition—considering how much he eats and drinks.

CLEOPATRA. Oh, you must not say common, earthly things about him; for I love him. He is a god.

CÆSAR. He is a great captain of horsemen, and swifter of foot than any other Roman.

CLEOPATRA. What is his real name?

CÆSAR [*puzzled*] His real name?

CLEOPATRA. Yes, I always call him Horus, because Horus is the most beautiful of our gods. But I want to know his real name.

CÆSAR. His name is Mark Antony.

CLEOPATRA [*musically*] Mark Antony, Mark Antony, Mark

Antony! What a beautiful name! [*She throws her arms round Cæsar's neck*]. Oh, how I love you for sending him to help my father! Did you love my father very much?

CÆSAR. No, my child; but your father, as you say, never worked. I always work. So when he lost his crown he had to promise me 16,000 talents to get it back for him.

CLEOPATRA. Did he ever pay you?

CÆSAR. Not in full.

CLEOPATRA. He was quite right: it was too dear. The whole world is not worth 16,000 talents.

CÆSAR. That is perhaps true, Cleopatra. Those Egyptians who work paid as much of it as he could drag from them. The rest is still due. But as I most likely shall not get it, I must go back to my work. So you must run away for a little and send my secretary to me.

CLEOPATRA [*coaxing*] No: I want to stay and hear you talk about Mark Antony.

CÆSAR. But if I do not get to work, Pothinus and the rest of them will cut us off from the harbor; and then the way from Rome will be blocked.

CLEOPATRA. No matter: I dont want you to go back to Rome.

CÆSAR. But you want Mark Antony to come from it.

CLEOPATRA [*springing up*] Oh yes, yes, yes: I forgot. Go quickly and work, Cæsar; and keep the way over the sea open for my Mark Antony. [*She runs out through the loggia, kissing her hand to Mark Antony across the sea*].

CÆSAR [*going briskly up the middle of the hall to the loggia steps*] Ho, Britannus. [*He is startled by the entry of a wounded Roman soldier, who confronts him from the upper step*]. What now?

SOLDIER [*pointing to his bandaged head*] This, Cæsar; and two of my comrades killed in the market place.

CÆSAR [*quiet, but attending*] Ay. Why?

SOLDIER. There is an army come to Alexandria, calling itself the Roman army.

CÆSAR. The Roman army of occupation. Ay?

SOLDIER. Commanded by one Achillas.

CÆSAR. Well?

SOLDIER. The citizens rose against us when the army entered the gates. I was with two others in the market place when the news came. They set upon us. I cut my way out; and here I am.

CÆSAR. Good. I am glad to see you alive. [*Rufio enters the loggia hastily, passing behind the soldier to look out through one of the arches at the quay beneath*]. Rufio: we are besieged.

RUFIO. What! Already?

CÆSAR. Now or tomorrow: what does it matter? We shall be besieged.

Britannus runs in.

BRITANNUS. Cæsar—

CÆSAR [*anticipating him*] Yes: I know. [*Rufio and Britannus come down the hall from the loggia at opposite sides, past Cæsar, who waits for a moment near the step to say to the soldier*] Comrade: give the word to turn out on the beach and stand by the boats. Get your wound attended to. Go. [*The soldier hurries out. Cæsar comes down the hall between Rufio and Britannus*] Rufio: we have some ships in the west harbor. Burn them.

RUFIO [*staring*] Burn them!!

CÆSAR. Take every boat we have in the east harbor, and seize the Pharos—that island with the lighthouse. Leave half our men behind to hold the beach and the quay outside this palace: that is the way home.

RUFIO [*disapproving strongly*] Are we to give up the city?

CÆSAR. We have not got it, Rufio. This palace we have; and—what is that building next door?

RUFIO. The theatre.

CÆSAR. We will have that too: it commands the strand. For the rest, Egypt for the Egyptians!

RUFIO. Well, you know best, I suppose. Is that all?

CÆSAR. That is all. Are those ships burnt yet?

RUFIO. Be easy: I shall waste no more time. [*He runs out*].

BRITANNUS. Cæsar: Pothinus demands speech of you. In my opinion he needs a lesson. His manner is most insolent.

CÆSAR. Where is he?

BRITANNUS. He waits without.

CÆSAR. Ho there! admit Pothinus.

Pothinus appears in the loggia, and comes down the hall very haughtily to Cæsar's left hand.

CÆSAR. Well, Pothinus?

POTHINUS. I have brought you our ultimatum, Cæsar.

CÆSAR. Ultimatum! The door was open: you should have gone out through it before you declared war. You are my prisoner now. [*He goes to the chair and loosens his toga*].

POTHINUS [*scornfully*] I your prisoner! Do you know that you are in Alexandria, and that King Ptolemy, with an army outnumbering your little troop a hundred to one, is in possession of Alexandria?

CÆSAR [*unconcernedly taking off his toga and throwing it on the chair*] Well, my friend, get out if you can. And tell your friends not to kill any more Romans in the market place. Otherwise my soldiers, who do not share my celebrated clemency, will probably kill you. Britannus: pass the word to the guard; and fetch my armor. [*Britannus runs out. Rufio returns*]. Well?

RUFIO [*pointing from the loggia to a cloud of smoke drifting over the harbor*] See there! [*Pothinus runs eagerly up the steps to look out*].

CÆSAR. What, ablaze already! Impossible!

RUFIO. Yes, five good ships, and a barge laden with oil grappled to each. But it is not my doing: the Egyptians have saved me the trouble. They have captured the west harbor.

CÆSAR [*anxiously*] And the east harbor? The lighthouse, Rufio?

RUFIO [*with a sudden splutter of raging ill usage, coming down to Cæsar and scolding him*] Can I embark a legion in five minutes? The first cohort is already on the beach. We can do no more. If you want faster work, come and do it yourself.

CÆSAR [*soothing him*] Good, good. Patience, Rufio, patience.

RUFIO. Patience! Who is impatient here, you or I? Would I be here, if I could not oversee them from that balcony?

CÆSAR. Forgive me, Rufio; and [*anxiously*] hurry them as much as—

He is interrupted by an outcry as of an old man in the extremity of misfortune. It draws near rapidly; and Theodotus rushes in, tearing his hair, and squeaking the most lamentable exclamations. Rufio steps back to stare at him, amazed at his frantic condition. Pothinus turns to listen.

THEODOTUS [*on the steps, with uplifted arms*] Horror unspeakable! Woe, alas! Help!

RUFIO. What now?

CÆSAR [*frowning*] Who is slain?

THEODOTUS. Slain! Oh, worse than the death of ten thousand men! Loss irreparable to mankind!

RUFIO. What has happened, man?

THEODOTUS [*rushing down the hall between them*] The fire has spread from your ships. The first of the seven wonders of the world perishes. The library of Alexandria is in flames.

RUFIO. Psha! [*Quite relieved, he goes up to the loggia and watches the preparations of the troops on the beach*].

CÆSAR. Is that all?

THEODOTUS [*unable to believe his senses*] All! Cæsar: will you go down to posterity as a barbarous soldier too ignorant to know the value of books?

CÆSAR. Theodotus: I am an author myself; and I tell you it is better that the Egyptians should live their lives than dream them away with the help of books.

THEODOTUS [*kneeling, with genuine literary emotion: the passion of the pedant*] Cæsar: once in ten generations of men, the world gains an immortal book.

CÆSAR [*inflexible*] If it did not flatter mankind, the common executioner would burn it.

THEODOTUS. Without history, death will lay you beside your meanest soldier.

CÆSAR. Death will do that in any case. I ask no better grave.

THEODOTUS. What is burning there is the memory of mankind.

CÆSAR. A shameful memory. Let it burn.

THEODOTUS [*wildly*] Will you destroy the past?

CÆSAR. Ay, and build the future with its ruins. [*Theodotus, in despair, strikes himself on the temples with his fists*]. But harken, Theodotus, teacher of kings: you who valued Pompey's head no more than a shepherd values an onion, and who now kneel to me, with tears in your old eyes, to plead for a few sheepskins scrawled with errors. I cannot spare you a man or a bucket of water just now; but you shall pass freely out of the palace. Now, away with you to Achillas; and borrow his legions to put out the fire. [*He hurries him to the steps*].

POTHINUS [*significantly*] You understand, Theodotus: I remain a prisoner.

THEODOTUS. A prisoner!

CÆSAR. Will you stay to talk whilst the memory of mankind is burning? [*Calling through the loggia*] Ho there! Pass Theodotus out. [*To Theodotus*] Away with you.

THEODOTUS [*To Pothinus*] I must go to save the library. [*He hurries out*].

CÆSAR. Follow him to gate, Pothinus. Bid him urge your people to kill no more of my soldiers, for your sake.

POTHINUS. My life will cost you dear if you take it, Cæsar. [*He goes out after Theodotus*].

Rufio, absorbed in watching the embarkation, does not notice the departure of the two Egyptians.

RUFIO [*shouting from the loggia to the beach*] All ready, there?

A CENTURION [*from below*] All ready. We wait for Cæsar.

CÆSAR. Tell them Cæsar is coming—the rogues! [*Calling*] Britannicus. [*This magniloquent version of his secretary's name is one of Cæsar's jokes. In later years it would have meant, quite seriously and officially, Conqueror of Britain*].

RUFIO [*calling down*] Push off, all except the longboat. Stand by it to embark, Cæsar's guard there. [*He leaves the balcony and comes down into the hall*]. Where are those Egyptians? Is this more clemency? Have you let them go?

CÆSAR [*chuckling*] I have let Theodotus go to save the library. We must respect literature, Rufio.

RUFIO [*raging*] Folly on folly's head! I believe if you could bring back all the dead of Spain, Gaul, and Thessaly to life, you would do it that we might have the trouble of fighting them over again.

CÆSAR. Might not the gods destroy the world if their only thought were to be at peace next year? [*Rufio, out of all patience, turns away in anger. Cæsar suddenly grips his sleeve, and adds slyly in his ear*] Besides, my friend: every Egyptian we imprison means imprisoning two Roman soldiers to guard him. Eh?

RUFIO. Agh! I might have known there was some fox's trick behind your fine talking. [*He gets away from Cæsar with an ill-humored shrug, and goes to the balcony for another look at the preparations; finally goes out*].

CÆSAR. Is Britannus asleep? I sent him for my armor an hour ago. [*Calling*] Britannicus, thou British islander. Britannicus!

Cleopatra runs in through the loggia with Cæsar's helmet and sword, snatched from Britannus, who follows her with a cuirass and greaves. They come down to Cæsar, she to his left hand, Britannus to his right.

CLEOPATRA. I am going to dress you, Cæsar. Sit down. [*He obeys*]. These Roman helmets are so becoming! [*She takes off his wreath*]. Oh! [*She bursts out laughing at him*].

CÆSAR. What are you laughing at?

CLEOPATRA. Youre bald [*beginning with a big B, and end-ing with a splutter*].

CÆSAR [*almost annoyed*] Cleopatra! [*He rises, for the convenience of Britannus, who puts the cuirass on him*].

CLEOPATRA. So that is why you wear the wreath—to hide it.

BRITANNUS. Peace, Egyptian: they are the bays of the conqueror. [*He buckles the cuirass*].

CLEOPATRA. Peace, thou: islander! [*To Cæsar*] You should rub your head with strong spirits of sugar, Cæsar. That will make it grow.

CÆSAR [*with a wry face*] Cleopatra: do you like to be reminded that you are very young?

CLEOPATRA [*pouting*] No.

CÆSAR [*sitting down again, and setting out his leg for Britannus, who kneels to put on his greaves*]. Neither do I like to be reminded that I am—middle aged. Let me give you ten of my superfluous years. That will make you 26, and leave me only—no matter. Is it a bargain?

CLEOPATRA. Agreed. 26, mind. [*She puts the helmet on him*]. Oh! How nice! You look only about 50 in it!

BRITANNUS [*looking up severely at Cleopatra*] You must not speak in this manner to Cæsar.

CLEOPATRA. Is it true that when Cæsar caught you on that island, you were painted all over blue?

BRITANNUS. Blue is the color worn by all Britons of good standing. In war we stain our bodies blue; so that though our enemies may strip us of our clothes and our lives, they cannot strip us of our respectability. [*He rises*].

CLEOPATRA [*with Cæsar's sword*] Let me hang this on. Now you look splendid. Have they made any statues of you in Rome?

CÆSAR. Yes, many statues.

CLEOPATRA. You must send for one and give it to me.

RUFIO [*coming back into the loggia, more impatient than ever*] Now Cæsar: have you done talking? The moment your foot is aboard there will be no holding our men back: the boats will race one another for the lighthouse.

CÆSAR [*drawing his sword and trying the edge*] Is this well set today, Britannicus? At Pharsalia it was as blunt as a barrel-hoop.

BRITANNUS. It will split one of the Egyptian's hairs today, Cæsar. I have set it myself.

CLEOPATRA [*suddenly throwing her arms in terror round Cæsar*] Oh, you are not really going into battle to be killed?

CÆSAR. No, Cleopatra. No man goes to battle to be killed.

CLEOPATRA. But they do get killed. My sister's husband was killed in battle. You must not go. Let him go [*pointing to Rufio. They all laugh at her*]. Oh please, please dont go. What will happen to me if you never come back?

CÆSAR [*gravely*] Are you afraid?

CLEOPATRA [*shrinking*] No.

CÆSAR [*with quiet authority*] Go to the balcony; and you shall see us take the Pharos. You must learn to look on battles. Go. [*She goes, downcast, and looks out from the balcony*]. That is well. Now, Rufio. March.

CLEOPATRA [*suddenly clapping her hands*] Oh, you will not be able to go!

CÆSAR. Why? What now?

CLEOPATRA. They are drying up the harbor with buckets —a multitude of soldiers—over there [*pointing out across the sea to her left*]—they are dipping up the water.

RUFIO [*hastening to look*] It is true. The Egyptian army! Crawling over the edge of the west harbor like locusts. [*With sudden anger he strides down to Cæsar*]. This is your accursed clemency, Cæsar. Theodotus has brought them.

CÆSAR [*delighted at his own cleverness*] I meant him to, Rufio. They have come to put out the fire. The library will keep them busy whilst we seize the lighthouse. Eh? [*He rushes out buoyantly through the loggia, followed by Britannus*].

RUFIO [*disgustedly*] More foxing! Agh! [*He rushes off. A*

shout from the soldiers announces the appearance of Cæsar below].

CENTURION [*below*] All aboard. Give way there. [*Another shout*].

CLEOPATRA [*waving her scarf through the loggia arch*] Goodbye, goodbye, dear Cæsar. Come back safe. Goodbye!

ACT III

The edge of the quay in front of the palace, looking out west over the east harbor of Alexandria to Pharos island, just to the end of which, and connected with it by a narrow mole, is the famous lighthouse, a gigantic square tower of white marble diminishing in size storey by storey to the top, on which stands a cresset beacon. The island is joined to the main land by the Heptastadium, a great mole or causeway five miles long bounding the harbor on the south.

In the middle of the quay a Roman sentinel stands on guard, pilum in hand, looking out to the lighthouse with strained attention, his left hand shading his eyes. The pilum is a stout wooden shaft $4\frac{1}{2}$ feet long, with an iron spit about three feet long fixed in it. The sentinel is so absorbed that he does not notice the approach from the north end of the quay of four Egyptian market porters carrying rolls of carpet, preceded by Ftatateeta and Apollodorus the Sicilian. Apollodorus is a dashing young man of about 24, handsome and debonair, dressed with deliberate æstheticism in the most delicate purples and dove greys, with ornaments of bronze, oxydized silver, and stones of jade and agate. His sword, designed as carefully as a medieval cross, has a blued blade shewing through an openwork scabbard of purple leather and filigree. The porters, conducted by Ftatateeta, pass along the quay behind the sentinel to the steps of the palace, where they put down their bales and squat on the ground. Apollodorus does not pass along with them: he halts, amused by the preoccupation of the sentinel.

APOLLODORUS [*calling to the sentinel*] Who goes there, eh?

SENTINEL [*starting violently and turning with his pilum at the charge, revealing himself as a small, wiry, sandy-haired, conscientious young man with an elderly face*] Whats this? Stand. Who are you?

APOLLODORUS. I am Apollodorus the Sicilian. Why, man, what are you dreaming of? Since I came through the lines beyond the theatre there, I have brought my caravan past three sentinels, all so busy staring at the lighthouse that not one of them challenged me. Is this Roman discipline?

SENTINEL. We are not here to watch the land but the sea. Cæsar has just landed on the Pharos. [*Looking at Ftatateeta*] What have you here? Who is this piece of Egyptian crockery?

FTATATEETA. Apollodorus: rebuke this Roman dog; and bid him bridle his tongue in the presence of Ftatateeta, the mistress of the Queen's household.

APOLLODORUS. My friend: this is a great lady, who stands high with Cæsar.

SENTINEL [*not at all impressed, pointing to the carpets*] And what is all this truck?

APOLLODORUS. Carpets for the furnishing of the Queen's apartments in the palace. I have picked them from the best carpets in the world; and the Queen shall choose the best of my choosing.

SENTINEL. So you are the carpet merchant?

APOLLODORUS [*hurt*] My friend: I am a patrician.

SENTINEL. A patrician! A patrician keeping a shop instead of following arms!

APOLLODORUS. I do not keep a shop. Mine is a temple of the arts. I am a worshipper of beauty. My calling is to choose beautiful things for beautiful queens. My motto is Art for Art's sake.

SENTINEL. That is not the password.

APOLLODORUS. It is a universal password.

SENTINEL. I know nothing about universal passwords. Either give me the password for the day or get back to your shop.

Ftatateeta, roused by his hostile tone, steals towards the edge of the quay with the step of a panther, and gets behind him.

APOLLODORUS. How if I do neither?

SENTINEL. Then I will drive this pilum through you.

APOLLODRUS. At your service, my friend. [*He draws his sword, and springs to his guard with unruffled grace*].

FTATATEETA [*suddenly seizing the sentinel's arms from behind*] Thrust your knife into the dog's throat, Apollodorus. [*The chivalrous Apollodorus laughingly shakes his head; breaks ground away from the sentinel towards the palace; and lowers his point*].

SENTINEL [*struggling vainly*] Curse on you! Let me go. Help ho!

FTATATEETA [*lifting him from the ground*] Stab the little Roman reptile. Spit him on your sword.

A couple of Roman soldiers, with a centurion, come running along the edge of the quay from the north end. They rescue their comrade, and throw off Ftatateeta, who is sent reeling away on the left hand of the sentinel.

CENTURION [*an unattractive man of fifty, short in his speech and manners, with a vinewood cudgel in his hand*] How now? What is all this?

FTATATEETA [*to Apollodorus*] Why did you not stab him? There was time!

APOLLODORUS. Centurion: I am here by order of the Queen to—

CENTURION [*interrupting him*] The Queen! Yes, yes: [*to the sentinel*] pass him in. Pass all these bazaar people in to the Queen, with their goods. But mind you pass no one out that you have not passed in—not even the Queen herself.

SENTINEL. This old woman is dangerous: she is as strong as three men. She wanted the merchant to stab me.

APOLLODORUS. Centurion: I am not a merchant. I am a patrician and a votary of art.

CENTURION. Is the woman your wife?

APOLLODORUS [*horrified*] No, no! [*Correcting himself politely*] Not that the lady is not a striking figure in her own way. But [*emphatically*] she is not my wife.

FTATATEETA [*to the centurion*] Roman: I am Ftatateeta, the mistress of the Queen's household.

CENTURION. Keep your hands off our men, mistress; or I will have you pitched into the harbor, though you were as strong as ten men. [*To his men*] To your posts: march! [*He returns with his men the way they came*].

FTATATEETA [*looking malignantly after him*] We shall see whom Isis loves best: her servant Ftatateeta or a dog of a Roman.

SENTINEL [*to Apollodorus, with a wave of his pilum towards the palace*] Pass in there; and keep your distance. [*Turning to Ftatateeta*] Come within a yard of me, you old crocodile; and I will give you this [*the pilum*] in your jaws.

CLEOPATRA [*calling from the palace*] Ftatateeta, Ftatateeta.

FTATATEETA [*looking up, scandalized*] Go from the window, go from the window. There are men here.

CLEOPATRA. I am coming down.

FTATATEETA [*distracted*] No, no. What are you dreaming of? O ye gods, ye gods! Apollodorus: bid your men pick up your bales; and in with me quickly.

APOLLODORUS. Obey the mistress of the Queen's household.

FTATATEETA [*impatiently, as the porters stoop to lift the bales*] Quick, quick: she will be out upon us. [*Cleopatra comes from the palace and runs across the quay to Ftatateeta*]. Oh that ever I was born!

CLEOPATRA [*eagerly*] Ftatateeta: I have thought of something. I want a boat—at once.

FTATATEETA. A boat! No, no: you cannot, Apollodorus: speak to the Queen.

APOLLODORUS [*gallantly*] Beautiful queen: I am Apollodorus the Sicilian, your servant, from the bazaar. I have brought you the three most beautiful Persian carpets in the world to choose from.

CLEOPATRA. I have no time for carpets today. Get me a boat.

FTATATEETA. What whim is this? You cannot go on the

water except in the royal barge.

APOLLODORUS. Royalty, Ftatateeta, lies not in the barge but in the Queen. [*To Cleopatra*] The touch of your majesty's foot on the gunwale of the meanest boat in the harbor will make it royal. [*He turns to the harbor and calls seaward*] Ho there, boatman! Pull in to the steps.

CLEOPATRA. Apollodorus: you are my perfect knight; and I will always buy my carpets through you. [*Apollodorus bows joyously. An oar appears above the quay; and the boatman, a bullet-headed, vivacious, grinning fellow, burnt almost black by the sun, comes up a flight of steps from the water on the sentinel's right, oar in hand, and waits at the top*]. Can you row, Apollodorus?

APOLLODORUS. My oars shall be your majesty's wings. Whither shall I row my Queen?

CLEOPATRA. To the lighthouse. Come. [*She makes for the steps*].

SENTINEL [*opposing her with his pilum at the charge*] Stand. You cannot pass.

CLEOPATRA [*flushing angrily*] How dare you? Do you know that I am the Queen?

SENTINEL. I have my orders. You cannot pass.

CLEOPATRA. I will make Cæsar have you killed if you do not obey me.

SENTINEL. He will do worse to me if I disobey my officer. Stand back.

CLEOPATRA. Ftatateeta: strangle him.

SENTINEL [*alarmed—looking apprehensively at Ftatateeta, and brandishing his pilum*] Keep off, there.

CLEOPATRA [*running to Apollodorus*] Apollodorus: make your slaves help us.

APOLLODORUS. I shall not need their help, lady. [*He draws his sword*]. Now, soldier: choose which weapon you will defend yourself with. Shall it be sword against pilum, or sword against sword?

SENTINEL. Roman against Sicilian, curse you. Take that.

[*He hurls his pilum at Apollodorus, who drops expertly on one knee. The pilum passes whizzing over his head and falls harmless. Apollodorus, with a cry of triumph, springs up and attacks the sentinel, who draws his sword and defends himself, crying*] Ho there, guard. Help!

Cleopatra, half frightened, half delighted, takes refuge near the palace, where the porters are squatting among the bales. The boatman, alarmed, hurries down the steps out of harm's way, but stops, with his head just visible above the edge of the quay, to watch the fight. The sentinel is handicapped by his fear of an attack in the rear from Ftatateeta. His swordsmanship, which is of rough and ready sort, is heavily taxed, as he has occasionally to strike at her to keep her off me between a blow and a guard with Apollodorus. The centurion returns with several soldiers. Apollodorus springs back towards Cleopatra as this reinforcement confronts him.

CENTURION [*coming to the sentinel's right hand*] What is this? What now?

SENTINEL [*panting*] I could do well enough by myself if it werent for the old woman. Keep her off me: that is all the help I need.

CENTURION. Make your report, soldier. What has happened?

FTATATEETA: Centurion: he would have slain the Queen.

SENTINEL: [*bluntly*] I would, sooner than let her pass. She wanted to take boat, and go—so she said—to the lighthouse. I stopped her, as I was ordered to; and she set this fellow on me.[*He goes to pick up his pilum and returns to his place with it*].

CENTURION [*turning to Cleopatra*] Cleopatra: I am loth to offend you; but without Cæsar's express order we dare not let you pass beyond the Roman lines.

APOLLODORUS. Well, Centurion; and has not the lighthouse been within the Roman lines since Cæsar landed there?

CLEOPATRA. Yes, yes. Answer that, if you can.

CENTURION [*to Apollodorus*] As for you, Apollodorus, you

may thank the gods that you are not nailed to the palace door with a pilum for your meddling.

APOLLODORUS [*urbanely*] My military friend, I was not born to be slain by so ugly a weapon. When I fall, it will be [*holding up his sword*] by this white queen of arms, the only weapon fit for an artist. And now that you are convinced that we do not want to go beyond the lines, let me finish killing your sentinel and depart with the Queen.

CENTURION [*as the sentinel makes an angry demonstration*] Peace there, Cleopatra: I must abide by my orders, and not by the subtleties of this Sicilian. You must withdraw into the palace and examine your carpets there.

CLEOPATRA [*pouting*] I will not: I am the Queen. Cæsar does not speak to me as you do. Have Cæsar's centurions changed manners with his scullions?

CENTURION [*sulkily*] I do my duty. That is enough for me.

APOLLODORUS. Majesty: when a stupid man is doing something he is ashamed of, he always declares that it is his duty.

CENTURION [*angry*] Apollodorus—

APOLLODORUS [*interrupting him with defiant elegance*] I will make amends for that insult with my sword at fitting time and place. Who says artist, says duellist. [*To Cleopatra*] Hear my counsel, star of the east. Until word comes to these soldiers from Cæsar himself, you are a prisoner. Let me go to him with a message from you, and a present; and before the sun has stooped half way to the arms of the sea, I will bring you back Cæsar's order of release.

CENTURION [*sneering at him*] And you will sell the Queen the present, no doubt.

APOLLODORUS. Centurion: the Queen shall have from me, without payment, as the unforced tribute of Sicilian taste to Egyptian beauty, the richest of these carpets for her present to Cæsar.

CLEOPATRA [*exultantly, to the centurion*] Now you see what an ignorant common creature you are!

CENTURION [*curtly*] Well, a fool and his wares are soon

parted. [*He turns to his men*] Two more men to this post here; and see that no one leaves the palace but this man and his merchandize. If he draws his sword again inside the lines, kill him. To your posts. March.

He goes out, leaving two auxiliary sentinels with the other.

APOLLODORUS [*with polite goodfellowship*] My friends: will you not enter the palace and bury our quarrel in a bowl of wine? [*He takes out his purse, jingling the coins in it*]. The Queen has presents for you all.

SENTINEL [*very sulky*] You heard our orders. Get about your business.

FIRST AUXILIARY. Yes: you ought to know better. Off with you.

SECOND AUXILIARY [*looking longingly at the purse—this sentinel is a hooknosed man, unlike his comrade, who is squab faced*] Do not tantalize a poor man.

APOLLODORUS [*to Cleopatra*] Pearl of Queens: the centurion is at hand; and the Roman soldier is incorruptible when his officer is looking. I must carry your word to Cæsar.

CLEOPATRA [*who has been meditating among the carpets*] Are these carpets very heavy?

APOLLODORUS. It matters not how heavy. There are plenty of porters.

CLEOPATRA. How do they put the carpets into boats? Do they throw them down?

APOLLODORUS. Not into small boats, majesty. It would sink them.

CLEOPATRA. Not into that man's boat, for instance? [*pointing to the boatman*].

APOLLODORUS. No. Too small.

CLEOPATRA. But you can take a carpet to Cæsar in it if I send one?

APOLLODORUS. Assuredly.

CLEOPATRA. And you will have it carried gently down the steps and take great care of it?

APOLLODORUS. Depend on me.

CLEOPATRA. Great, great care?

APOLLODORUS. More than of my own body.

CLEOPATRA. You will promise me not to let the porters drop it or throw it about?

APOLLODORUS. Place the most delicate glass goblet in the palace in the heart of the roll, Queen; and if it be broken, my head shall pay for it.

CLEOPATRA. Good. Come, Ftatateeta. [*Ftatateeta comes to her. Apollodorus offers to squire them into the palace*]. No, Apollodorus, you must not come. I will choose a carpet for myself. You must wait here. [*She runs into the palace*].

APOLLODORUS [*to the porters*] Follow this lady [*indicating Ftatateeta*] and obey her.

The porters rise and take up their bales.

FTATATEETA [*addressing the porters as if they were vermin*] This way. And take your shoes off before you put your feet on those stairs.

She goes in, followed by the porters with the carpets. Meanwhile Apollodorus goes to the edge of the quay and looks out over the harbor. The sentinels keep their eyes on him malignantly.

APOLLODORUS [*addressing the sentinel*] My friend—

SENTINEL [*rudely*] Silence there.

FIRST AUXILIARY. Shut your muzzle, you.

SECOND AUXILIARY [*in a half whisper, glancing apprehensively towards the north end of the quay*] Cant you wait a bit?

APOLLODORUS. Patience, worthy three-headed donkey. [*They mutter ferociously; but he is not at all intimidated*]. Listen: were you set here to watch me, or to watch the Egyptians?

SENTINEL. We know our duty.

APOLLODORUS. Then why dont you do it? There is something going on over there [*pointing southwestward to the mole*].

SENTINEL [*sulkily*] I do not need to be told what to do by the like of you.

APOLLODORUS. Blockhead. [*He begins shouting*] Ho there, Centurion. Hoiho!

SENTINEL. Curse your meddling. [*Shouting*] Hoiho! Alarm! Alarm!

FIRST AND SECOND AUXILIARIES. Alarm! alarm! Hoiho!

The Centurion comes running in with his guard.

CENTURION. What now? Has the old woman attacked you again? [*Seeing Apollodorus*] Are you here still?

APOLLODORUS [*pointing as before*] See there. The Egyptians are moving. They are going to recapture the Pharos. They will attack by sea and land: by land along the great mole; by sea from the west harbor. Stir yourselves, my military friends: the hunt is up. [*A clangor of trumpets from several points along the quay*]. Aha! I told you so.

CENTURION [*quickly*] The two extra men pass the alarm to the south posts. One man keep guard here. The rest with me—quick.

The two auxiliary sentinels run off to the south. The centurion and his guard run off northward; and immediately afterwards the bucina sounds. The four porters come from the palace carrying a carpet, followed by Ftatateeta.

SENTINEL [*handling his pilum apprehensively*] You again! [*The porters stop*].

FTATATEETA. Peace, Roman fellow: you are now single-handed. Apollodorus: this carpet is Cleopatra's present to Cæsar. It has rolled up in it ten precious goblets of the thinnest Iberian crystal, and a hundred eggs of the sacred blue pigeon. On your honor, let not one of them be broken.

APOLLODORUS. On my head be it! [*To the porters*] Into the boat with them carefully.

The porters carry the carpet to the steps.

FIRST PORTER [*looking down at the boat*] Beware what you do, sir. Those eggs of which the lady speaks must weigh more than a pound apiece. This boat is too small for such a load.

BOATMAN [*excitedly rushing up the steps*] Oh thou injurious porter! Oh thou unnatural son of a she-camel! [*To Apollodorus*] My boat, sir, hath often carried five men. Shall it not carry your lordship and a bale of pigeon's eggs? [*To the porter*] Thou mangey dromedary, the gods shall punish thee for this envious wickedness.

FIRST PORTER [*stolidly*] I cannot quit this bale now to beat these; but another day I will lie in wait for thee.

APOLLODORUS [*going between them*] Peace there. If the boat were but a single plank, I would get to Cæsar on it.

FTATATEETA [*anxiously*] In the name of the gods, Apollodorus, run no risks with that bale.

APOLLODORUS. Fear not, thou venerable grotesque: I guess its great worth. [*To the porters*] Down with it, I say; and gently; or ye shall eat nothing but stick for ten days.

The boatman goes down the steps, followed by the porters with the bale: Ftatateeta and Apollodorus watching from the edge.

APOLLODORUS. Gently, my sons, my children—[*with sudden alarm*] gently, ye dogs. Lay it level in the stern—so—tis well.

FTATATEETA [*screaming down at one of the porters*] Do not step on it, do not step on it. Oh thou brute beast!

FIRST PORTER [*ascending*] Be not excited, mistress: all is well.

FTATATEETA [*panting*] All well! Oh, thou hast given my heart a turn! [*She clutches her side, gasping*].

The four porters have now come up and are waiting at the stairhead to be paid.

APOLLODORUS. Here, ye hungry ones. [*He gives money to the first porter, who holds it in his hand to shew to the others. They crowd greedily to see how much it is, quite prepared, after the Eastern fashion, to protest to heaven against their patron's stinginess. But his liberality overpowers them*].

FIRST PORTER. O bounteous prince!

SECOND PORTER. O lord of the bazaar!

THIRD PORTER. O favored of the gods!

FOURTH PORTER. O father to all the porters of the market.

SENTINEL [*enviously, threatening them fiercely with his pilum*] Hence, dogs: off. Out of this. [*They fly before him northward along the quay*].

APOLLODORUS. Farewell, Ftatateeta. I shall be at the lighthouse before the Egyptians. [*He descends the steps*].

FTATATEETA. The gods speed thee and protect my nursling!

The sentry returns from chasing the porters and looks down at the boat, standing near the stairhead lest Ftatateeta should attempt to escape.

APOLLODORUS [*from beneath, as the boat moves off*] Farewell, valiant pilum pitcher.

SENTINEL. Farewell, shopkeeper.

APOLLODORUS. Ha, ha! Pull, thou brave boatman, pull. Soho-o-o-o-o! [*He begins to sing in barcarolle measure to the rhythm of the oars*]

> My heart, my heart, spread out thy wings:
> Shake off thy heavy load of love—

Give me the oars, O son of a snail.

SENTINEL [*threatening Ftatateeta*] Now mistress: back to your henhouse. In with you.

FTATATEETA [*falling on her knees and stretching her hands over the waters*] Gods of the seas, bear her safely to the shore!

SENTINEL. Bear who safely? What do you mean?

FTATATEETA [*looking darkly at him*] Gods of Egypt and of Vengeance, let this Roman fool be beaten like a dog by his captain for suffering her to be taken over the waters.

SENTINEL. Accursed one: is she then in the boat? [*He calls over the sea*] Hoiho, there, boatman! Hoiho!

APOLLODORUS [*singing in the distance*]

My heart, my heart, be whole and free:
Love is thine only enemy.

Meanwhile Rufio, the morning's fighting done, sits munching dates on a faggot of brushwood outside the door of the lighthouse, which towers gigantic to the clouds on his left. His helmet, full of dates, is between his knees; and a leathern bottle of wine is by his side. Behind him the great stone pedestal of the lighthouse is shut in from the open sea by a low stone parapet, with a couple of steps in the middle to the broad coping. A huge chain with a hook hangs down from the lighthouse crane above his head. Faggots like the one he sits on lie beneath it ready to be drawn up to feed the beacon.

Cæsar is standing on the step at the parapet looking out anxiously, evidently ill at ease. Britannus comes out of the lighthouse door.

RUFIO. Well, my British islander. Have you been up to the top?

BRITANNUS. I have. I reckon it at 200 feet high.

RUFIO. Anybody up there?

BRITANNUS. One elderly Tyrian to work the crane; and his son, a well conducted youth of 14.

RUFIO [*looking at the chain*] What! An old man and a boy work that! Twenty men, you mean.

BRITANNUS. Two only, I assure you. They have counterweights, and a machine with boiling water in it which I do not understand: it is not of British design. They use it to haul up barrels of oil and faggots to burn in the brazier on the roof.

RUFIO. But—

BRITANNUS. Excuse me: I came down because there are messengers coming along the mole to us from the island. I must see what their business is. [*He hurries out past the lighthouse*].

CÆSAR [*coming away from the parapet, shivering and out*

of sorts] Rufio: this has been a mad expedition. We shall be beaten. I wish I knew how our men are getting on with that barricade across the great mole.

RUFIO [*angrily*] Must I leave my food and go starving to bring you a report?

CÆSAR [*soothing him nervously*] No, Rufio, no. Eat, my son, eat. [*He takes another turn, Rufio chewing dates meanwhile*]. The Egyptians cannot be such fools as not to storm the barricade and swoop down on us here before it is finished. It is the first time I have ever run an avoidable risk. I should not have come to Egypt.

RUFIO. An hour ago you were all for victory.

CÆSAR [*apologetically*] Yes: I was a fool—rash, Rufio—boyish.

RUFIO. Boyish! Not a bit of it. Here [*offering him a handful of dates*]. What are these for?

RUFIO. To eat. Thats whats the matter with you. When a man comes to your age, he runs down before his midday meal. Eat and drink; and then have another look at our chances.

CÆSAR [*taking the dates*] My age! [*He shakes his head and bites a date*]. Yes, Rufio: I am an old man—worn out now —true, quite true. [*He gives way to melancholy contemplation, and eats another date*]. Achillas is still in his prime: Ptolemy is a boy. [*He eats another date, and plucks up a little*]. Well, every dog has his day; and I have had mine: I cannot complain. [*With sudden cheerfulness*] These dates are not bad, Rufio. [*Britannus returns, greatly excited, with a leathern bag. Cæsar is himself again in a moment*]. What now?

BRITANNUS [*triumphantly*] Our brave Rhodian mariners have captured a treasure. There! [*He throws the bag down at Cæsar's feet*]. Our enemies are delivered into our hands.

CÆSAR. In that bag?

BRITANNUS. Wait till you hear, Cæsar. This bag contains all

the letters which have passed between Pompey's party and the army of occupation here.

CÆSAR. Well?

BRITTANUS [*impatient of Cæsar's slowness to grasp the situation*] Well, we shall now know who your foes are. The name of every man who has plotted against you since you crossed the Rubicon may be in these papers, for all we know.

CÆSAR. Put them in the fire.

BRITANNUS. Put them—[*he gasps*]!!!!

CÆSAR. In the fire. Would you have me waste the next three years of my life of proscribing and condemning men who will be my friends when I have proved that my friendship is worth more than Pompey's was—than Cato's is. O incorrigible British islander: am I a bull dog, to seek quarrels merely to shew how stubborn my jaws are?

BRITANNUS. But your honor—the honor of Rome.

CÆSAR. I do not make human sacrifices to my honor, as your Druids do. Since you will not burn these, at least I can drown them. [*He picks up the bag and throws it over the parapet into the sea*].

BRITANNUS. Cæsar: this is mere eccentricity. Are traitors to be allowed to go free for the sake of a paradox?

RUFIO [*rising*] Cæsar: when the islander has finished preaching, call me again. I am going to have a look at the boiling water machine. [*He goes into the lighthouse*].

BRITANNUS [*with genuine feeling*] O Cæsar, my great master, if I could but persuade you to regard life seriously, as men do in my country!

CÆSAR. Do they truly do so, Britannus?

BRITANNUS. Have you not been there? Have you not seen them? What Briton speaks as you do in your moments of levity? What Briton neglects to attend the services at the sacred grove? What Briton wears clothes of many colors as you do, instead of plain blue, as all solid, well esteemed men should? These are moral questions with us.

CÆSAR. Well, well, my friend: some day I shall settle down and have a blue toga, perhaps. Meanwhile, I must get on as best I can in my flippant Roman way. [*Apollodorus comes past the lighthouse*]. What now?

BRITANNUS [*turning quickly, and challenging the stranger with official haughtiness*] What is this? Who are you? How did you come here?

APOLLODORUS. Calm yourself, my friend: I am not going to eat you. I have come by boat, from Alexandria, with precious gifts for Cæsar.

CÆSAR. From Alexandria!

BRITANNUS [*severely*] This is Cæsar, sir.

RUFIO [*appearing at the lighthouse door*] Whats the matter now?

APOLLODORUS. Hail, great Cæsar! I am Apollodorus the Sicilian, an artist.

BRITANNUS. An artist! Why have they admitted this vagabond?

CÆSAR. Peace, man. Apollodorus is a famous patrician amateur.

BRITANNUS [*disconcerted*] I crave the gentleman's pardon. [*To Cæsar*] I understood him to say that he was a professional. [*Somewhat out of countenance, he allows Apollodorus to approach Cæsar, changing places with him. Rufio, after looking Apollodorus up and down with marked disparagement, goes to the other side of the platform*].

CÆSAR. You are welcome, Apollodorus. What is your business?

APOLLODORUS. First, to deliver to you a present from the Queen of Queens.

CÆSAR. Who is that?

APOLLODORUS. Cleopatra of Egypt.

CÆSAR [*taking him into his confidence in his most winning manner*] Apollodorus: this is no time for playing with presents. Pray you, go back to the Queen, and tell her that if all goes well I shall return to the palace this evening.

APOLLODORUS. Cæsar: I cannot return. As I approached the lighthouse, some fool threw a great leathern bag into the sea. It broke the nose of my boat; and I had hardly time to get myself and my charge to the shore before the poor little cockleshell sank.

CÆSAR. I am sorry, Apollodorus. The fool shall be rebuked. Well, well: what have you brought me? The Queen will be hurt if I do not look at it.

RUFIO. Have we time to waste on this trumpery? The Queen is only a child.

CÆSAR. Just so: that is why we must not disappoint her. What is the present, Apollodorus?

APOLLODORUS. Cæsar: it is a Persian carpet—a beauty! And in it are—so I am told—pigeons' eggs and crystal goblets and fragile precious things. I dare not for my head have it carried up that narrow ladder from the causeway.

RUFIO. Swing it up by the crane, then. We will send the eggs to the cook; drink our wine from the goblets; and the carpet will make a bed for Cæsar.

APOLLODORUS. The crane! Cæsar: I have sworn to tender this bale of carpet as I tender my own life.

CÆSAR [cheerfully] Then let them swing you up at the same time; and if the chain breaks, you and the pigeons' eggs will perish together. [He goes to the chain and looks up along it, examining it curiously].

APOLLODORUS [to Britannus] Is Cæsar serious?

BRITANNUS. His manner is frivolous because he is an Italian; but he means what he says.

APOLLODORUS. Serious or not, he spake well. Give me a squad of soldiers to work the crane.

BRITANNUS. Leave the crane to me. Go and await the descent of the chain.

APOLLODORUS. Good. You will presently see me there [turning to them all and pointing with an eloquent gesture to the sky above the parapet] rising like the sun with my treasure.

He goes back the way he came. Britannus goes into the lighthouse.

RUFIO [*ill-humoredly*] Are you really going to wait here for this foolery, Cæsar?

CÆSAR [*backing away from the crane as it gives signs of working*] Why not?

RUFIO. The Egyptians will let you know why not if they have the sense to make a rush from the shore end of the mole before our barricade is finished. And here we are waiting like children to see a carpet full of pigeons' eggs.

The chain rattles, and is drawn up high enough to clear the parapet. It then swings round out of sight behind the lighthouse.

CÆSAR. Fear not, my son Rufio. When the first Egyptian takes his first step along the mole, the alarm will sound; and we two will reach the barricade from our end before the Egyptians reach it from their end—we two, Rufio: I, the old man, and you, his biggest boy. And the old man will be there first. So peace; and give me some more dates.

APOLLODORUS [*from the causeway below*] Soho, haul away. So-ho-o-o-o! [*The chain is drawn up and comes round again from behind the lighthouse. Apollodorus is swinging in the air with his bale of carpet at the end of it. He breaks into song as he soars above the parapet*]

> Aloft, aloft, behold the blue
> That never shone in woman's eyes-

Easy there: stop her. [*He ceases to rise*]. Further round! [*The chain comes forward above the platform*].

RUFIO [*calling up*] Lower away there. [*The chain and its load begin to descend*].

APOLLODORUS [*calling up*] Gently—slowly—mind the eggs.

RUFIO [*calling up*] Easy there—slowly—slowly.

Apollodorus and the bale are deposited safely on the flags in the middle of the platform. Rufio and Cæsar help Apollodorus to cast off the chain from the bale.

RUFIO. Haul up.

The chain rises clear of their heads with a rattle. Britannus comes from the lighthouse and helps them to uncord the carpet.

APOLLODORUS [*when the cords are loose*] Stand off, my friends: let Cæsar see. [*He throws the carpet open*].

RUFIO. Nothing but a heap of shawls. Where are the pigeons' eggs?

APOLLODORUS. Approach, Cæsar; and search for them among the shawls.

RUFIO [*drawing his sword*] Ha, treachery! Keep back, Cæsar: I saw the shawl move: there is something alive there.

BRITANNUS [*drawing his sword*] It is a serpent.

APOLLODORUS. Dares Cæsar thrust his hand into the sack where the serpent moves?

RUFIO [*turning on him*] Treacherous dog—

CÆSAR. Peace. Put up your swords. Apollodorus: your serpent seems to breathe very regularly. [*He thrusts his hand under the shawls and draws out a bare arm*]. This is a pretty little snake.

RUFIO [*drawing out the other arm*] Let us have the rest of you.

They pull Cleopatra up by the wrists into a sitting position. Britannus, scandalized, sheathes his sword with a drive of protest.

CLEOPATRA [*gasping*] Oh, I'm smothered. Oh, Cæsar, a man stood on me in the boat; and a great sack of something fell upon me out of the sky; and then the boat sank; and then I was swung up into the air and bumped down.

CÆSAR [*petting her as she rises and takes refuge on his breast*] Well, never mind: here you are safe and sound at last.

RUFIO. Ay; and now that she is here, what are we to do with her?

BRITANNUS. She cannot stay here, Cæsar, without the companionship of some matron.

CLEOPATRA [*jealously, to Cæsar, who is obviously perplexed*] Arnt you glad to see me?

CÆSAR. Yes, yes; I am very glad. But Rufio is very angry; and Britannus is shocked.

CLEOPATRA [*contemptuously*] You can have their heads cut off, can you not?

CÆSAR. They would not be so useful with their heads cut off as they are now, my sea bird.

RUFIO [*to Cleopatra*] We shall have to go away presently and cut some of your Egyptians' heads off. How will you like being left here with the chance of being captured by that little brother of yours if we are beaten?

CLEOPATRA. But you mustnt leave me alone. Cæsar: you will not leave me alone, will you?

RUFIO. What! not when the trumpet sounds and all our lives depend on Cæsar's being at the barricade before the Egyptians reach it? Eh?

CLEOPATRA. Let them lose their lives: they are only soldiers.

CÆSAR [*gravely*] Cleopatra: when that trumpet sounds, we must take every man his life in his hand, and throw it in the face of Death. And of my soldiers who have trusted me there is not one whose hand I shall not hold more sacred than your head. [*Cleopatra is overwhelmed. Her eyes fill with tears*]. Apollodorus: you must take her back to the palace.

APOLLODORUS. Am I a dolphin, Cæsar, to cross the seas with young ladies on my back? My boat is sunk: all yours are either at the barricade or have returned to the city. I will hail one if I can: that is all I can do. [*He goes back to the causeway*].

CLEOPATRA [*struggling with her tears*] It does not matter. I will not go back. Nobody cares for me.

CÆSAR. Cleopatra—

CLEOPATRA. You want me to be killed.

CÆSAR [*still more gravely*] My poor child: your life matters little here to anyone but yourself. [*She gives way al-*

together at this, casting herself down on the faggots weeping. Suddenly a great tumult is heard in the distance, bucinas and trumpets sounding through a storm of shouting. Britannus rushes to the parapet and looks along the mole. Cæsar and Rufio turn to one another with quick intelligence].

CÆSAR. Come, Rufio.

CLEOPATRA [*scrambling to her knees and clinging to him*]. No no. Do not leave me, Cæsar. [*He snatches his skirt from her clutch*]. Oh!

BRITANNUS [*from the parapet*] Cæsar: we are cut off. The Egyptians have landed from the west harbor between us and the barricade!!!

RUFIO [*running to see*] Curses! It is true. We are caught like rats in a trap.

CÆSAR [*ruthfully*] Rufio, Rufio: my men at the barricade are between the sea party and the shore party. I have murdered them.

RUFIO [*coming back from the parapet to Cæsar's right hand*] Ay: that comes of fooling with this girl here.

APOLLODORUS [*coming up quickly from the causeway*] Look over the parapet, Cæsar.

CÆSAR. We have looked, my friend. We must defend ourselves here.

APOLLODORUS. I have thrown the ladder into the sea. They cannot get in without it.

RUFIO. Ay; and we cannot get out. Have you thought of that?

APOLLODORUS. Not get out! Why not? You have ships in the east harbor.

BRITANNUS [*hopefully, at the parapet*] The Rhodian galleys are standing in towards us already. [*Cæsar quickly joins Britannus at the parapet*].

RUFIO [*to Apollodorus, impatiently*] And by what road are we to walk to the galleys, pray?

APOLLODORUS [*with gay, defiant rhetoric*] By the road that leads everywhere—the diamond path of the sun and moon.

Have you never seen the child's shadow play of The Broken Bridge? "Ducks and geese with ease get over"—eh? [*He throws away his cloak and cap, and binds his sword on his back*].

RUFIO. What are you talking about?

APOLLODORUS. I will shew you. [*Calling to Britannus*] How far off is the nearest galley?

BRITANNUS. Fifty fathom.

CÆSAR. No, no: they are further off than they seem in this clear air to your British eyes. Nearly quarter of a mile, Apollodorus.

APOLLODORUS. Good. Defend yourselves here until I send you a boat from that galley.

RUFIO. Have you wings, perhaps?

APOLLODORUS. Water wings, soldier. Behold!

He runs up the steps between Cæsar and Britannus to the coping of the parapet; springs into the air; and plunges head foremost into the sea.

CÆSAR [*like a schoolboy—wildly excited*] Bravo, bravo! [*Throwing off his cloak*] By Jupiter, I will do that too.

RUFIO [*seizing him*] You are mad. You shall not.

CÆSAR. Why not? Can I not swim as well as he?

RUFIO [*frantic*] Can an old fool dive and swim like a young one? He is twenty-five and you are fifty.

CÆSAR [*breaking loose from Rufio*] Old!!!

BRITANNUS [*shocked*] Rufio: you forget yourself.

CÆSAR. I will race you to the galley for a week's pay, father Rufio.

CLEOPATRA. But me! me!! me!!! what is to become of me?

CÆSAR. I will carry you on my back to the galley like a dolphin. Rufio: when you see me rise to the surface, throw her in: I will answer for her. And then in with you after her, both of you.

CLEOPATRA. No, no, NO. I shall be drowned.

BRITANNUS. Cæsar: I am a man and a Briton, not a fish. I must have a boat. I cannot swim.

CLEOPATRA. Neither can I.

CÆSAR [to Britannus] Stay here, then, alone, until I re-capture the lighthouse: I will not forget you. Now, Rufio.

RUFIO. You have made up your mind to this folly?

CÆSAR. The Egyptians have made it up for me. What else is there to do? And mind where you jump: I do not want to get your fourteen stone in the small of my back as I come up. [He runs up the steps and stands on the coping].

BRITANNUS [anxiously] One last word, Cæsar. Do not let yourself be seen in the fashionable part of Alexandria until you have changed your clothes.

CÆSAR [calling over the sea] Ho, Apollodorus: [he points skyward and quotes the barcarolle]

The white upon the blue above—

APOLLODORUS [swimming in the distance]

Is purple on the green below—

CÆSAR [exultantly] Aha! [He plunges into the sea].

CLEOPATRA [running excitedly to the steps] Oh, let me see. He will be drowned [Rufio seizes her]—Ah—ah—ah—ah! [He pitches her screaming into the sea. Rufio and Britannus roar with laughter].

RUFIO [looking down after her]. He has got her. [To Britannus] Hold the fort, Briton. Cæsar will not forget you. [He springs off].

BRITANNUS [running to the steps to watch them as they swim] All safe, Rufio?

RUFIO [swimming] All safe.

CÆSAR [swimming further off] Take refuge up there by the beacon; and pile the fuel on the trap door, Britannus.

BRITANNUS [calling in reply] I will first do so, and then commend myself to my country's gods. [A sound of cheering from the sea. Britannus gives full vent to his excitement]. The boat has reached him: Hip, hip, hip, hurrah!

ACT IV

Cleopatra's sousing in the east harbor of Alexandria was in October 48 B.C. In March 47 she is passing the afternoon in her boudoir in the palace, among a bevy of her ladies, listening to a slave girl who is playing the harp in the middle of the room. The harpist's master, an old musician, with a lined face, prominent brows, white beard, moustache and eyebrows twisted and horned at the ends, and a consciously keen and pretentious expression, is squatting on the floor close to her on her right, watching her performance. Ftatateeta is in attendance near the door, in front of a group of female slaves. Except the harp player all are seated: Cleopatra in a chair opposite the door on the other side of the room; the rest on the ground. Cleopatra's ladies are all young, the most conspicuous being Charmian and Iras, her favorites. Charmian is a hatchet faced, terra cotta colored little goblin, swift in her movements, and neatly finished at the hands and feet. Iras is a plump, goodnatured creature, rather fatuous, with a profusion of red hair, and a tendency to giggle on the slightest provocation.

CLEOPATRA. Can I—

FTATATEETA [*insolently, to the player*] Peace, thou! The Queen speaks. [*The player stops*].

CLEOPATRA [*to the old musician*] I want to learn to play the harp with my own hands. Cæsar loves music. Can you teach me?

MUSICIAN. Assuredly I and no one else can teach the queen. Have I not discovered the lost method of the ancient Egyptians, who could make a pyramid tremble by touching a bass string? All the other teachers are quacks: I have exposed them repeatedly.

CLEOPATRA. Good: you shall teach me. How long will it take?

MUSICIAN. Not very long: only four years. Your Majesty must first become proficient in the philosophy of Pythagoras.

CLEOPATRA. Has she [*indicating the slave*] become proficient in the philosophy of Pythagoras?

MUSICIAN. Oh, she is but a slave. She learns as a dog learns.

CLEOPATRA. Well, then, I will learn as a dog learns; for she plays better than you. You shall give me a lesson every day for a fortnight. [*The musician hastily scrambles to his feet and bows profoundly*]. After that, whenever I strike a false note you shall be flogged; and if I strike so many that there is not time to flog you, you shall be thrown into the Nile to feed the crocodiles. Give the girl a piece of gold; and send them away.

MUSICIAN [*much taken aback*] But true art will not be thus forced.

FTATATEETA [*pushing him out*] What is this? Answering the Queen, forsooth. Out with you.

He is pushed out by Ftatateeta, the girl following with her harp, amid the laughter of the ladies and slaves.

CLEOPATRA. Now, can any of you amuse me? Have you any stories or any news?

IRAS. Ftatateeta—

CLEOPATRA. Oh, Ftatateeta, Ftatateeta, always Ftatateeta. Some new tale to set me against her.

IRAS. No: this time Ftatateeta has been virtuous. [*All the ladies laugh—not the slaves*]. Pothinus has been trying to bribe her to let him speak with you.

CLEOPATRA [*wrathfully*] Ha! you all sell audiences with me, as if I saw whom you please, and not whom I please. I should like to know how much of her gold piece that harp girl will have to give up before she leaves the palace.

IRAS. We can easily find out that for you.

The ladies laugh.

CLEOPATRA [*frowning*] You laugh; but take care, take care. I will find out some day how to make myself served as Cæsar is served.

CHARMIAN. Old hooknose! [*They laugh again*].

CLEOPATRRA [*revolted*] Silence. Charmian: do not you be a silly little Egyptian fool. Do you know why I allow you all to chatter impertinently just as you please, instead of treating you as Ftatateeta would treat you if she were Queen?

CHARMIAN. Because you try to imitate Cæsar in everything; and he lets everybody say what they please to him.

CLEOPATRA. No; but because I asked him one day why he did so; and he said "Let your women talk; and you will learn something from them." What have I to learn from them? I said. "What they are," said he; and oh! you should have seen his eye as he said it. You would have curled up, you shallow things. [*They laugh. She turns fiercely on Iras*]. At whom are you laughing—at me or at Cæsar?

IRAS. At Cæsar.

CLEOPATRA. If you were not a fool, you would laugh at me; and if you were not a coward you would not be afraid to tell me so. [*Ftatateeta returns*]. Ftatateeta: they tell me that Pothinus has offered you a bribe to admit him to my presence.

FTATATEETA [*protesting*] Now by my father's gods—

CLEOPATRA [*cutting her short despotically*] Have I not told you not to deny things? You would spend the day calling your father's gods to witness to your virtues if I let you. Go take the bribe; and bring in Pothinus. [*Ftatateeta is about to reply*]. Dont answer me. Go.

Ftatateeta goes out; and Cleopatra rises and begins to prowl to and fro between her chair and the door, meditating. All rise and stand.

IRAS [*as she relunctantly rises*] Heigho! I wish Cæsar were back in Rome.

CLEOPATRA [*threateningly*] It will be a bad day for you all when he goes. Oh, if I were not ashamed to let him see that I am as cruel at heart as my father, I would make you repent that speech! Why do you wish him away?

CHARMIAN. He makes you so terribly prosy and serious and

learned and philosophical. It is worse than being religious, at our ages. [*The ladies laugh*].

CLEOPATRA. Cease that endless cackling, will you. Hold your tongues.

CHARMIAN [*with mock resignation*] Well, well: we must try to live up to Cæsar.

They laugh again. Cleopatra rages silently as she continues to prowl to and fro. Ftatateeta comes back with Pothinus, who halts on the threshold.

FTATATEETA [*at the door*] Pothinus craves the ear of the—

CLEOPATRA. There, there: that will do: let him come in. [*She resumes her seat. All sit down except Pothinus, who advances to the middle of the room. Ftatateeta takes her former place*]. Well, Pothinus: what is the latest news from your rebel friends?

POTHINUS [*haughtily*] I am no friend of rebellion. And a prisoner does not receive news.

CLEOPATRA. You are no more a prisoner than I am—than Cæsar is. These six months we have been besieged in this palace by my subjects. You are allowed to walk on the beach among the soldiers. Can I go further myself, or can Cæsar?

POTHINUS. You are but a child, Cleopatra, and do not understand these matters.

The ladies laugh. Cleopatra looks inscrutably at him.

CHARMIAN. I see you do not know the latest news, Pothinus.

POTHINUS. What is that?

CHARMIAN. That Cleopatra is no longer a child. Shall I tell you how to grow much older, and much, much wiser in one day?

POTHINUS. I should prefer to grow wiser without growing older.

CHARMIAN. Well, go up to the top of the lighthouse; and get somebody to take you by the hair and throw you into the sea. [*The ladies laugh*].

CLEOPATRA. She is right, Pothinus: you will come to the

shore with much conceit washed out of you. [*The ladies laugh. Cleopatra rises impatiently*]. Begone, all of you. I will speak with Pothinus alone. Drive them out, Ftatateeta. [*They run out laughing. Ftatateeta shuts the door on them*]. What are you waiting for?

FTATATEETA. It is not meet that the Queen remain alone with—

CLEOPATRA [*interrupting her*] Ftatateeta: must I sacrifice you to your father's gods to teach you that *I* am Queen of Egypt, and not you?

FTATATEETA [*indignantly*] You are like the rest of them. You want to be what these Romans call a New Woman. [*She goes out, banging the door*].

CLEOPATRA [*sitting down again*] Now, Pothinus: why did you bribe Ftatateeta to bring you hither?

POTHINUS [*studying her gravely*] Cleopatra: what they tell me is true. You are changed.

CLEOPATRA. Do you speak with Cæsar every day for six months: and you will be changed.

POTHINUS. It is the common talk that you are infatuated with this old man?

CLEOPATRA. Infatuated? What does that mean? Made foolish, is it not? Oh no: I wish I were.

POTHINUS. You wish you were made foolish! How so?

CLEOPATRA. When I was foolish, I did what I liked, except when Ftatateeta beat me; and even then I cheated her and did it by stealth. Now that Cæsar has made me wise, it is no use my liking or disliking: I do what must be done, and have no time to attend to myself. That is not happiness; but it is greatness. If Cæsar were gone, I think I could govern the Egyptians; for what Cæsar is to me, I am to the fools around me.

POTHINUS [*looking hard at her*] Cleopatra: this may be the vanity of youth.

CLEOPATRA. No, no: it is not that I am so clever, but that the others are so stupid.

POTHINUS [*musingly*] Truly, that is the great secret.

CLEOPATRA. Well, now tell me what you came to say?

POTHINUS [*embarrassed*] I! Nothing.

CLEOPATRA. Nothing!

POTHINUS. At least—to beg for my liberty: that is all.

CLEOPATRA. For that you would have knelt to Cæsar. No, Pothinus: you came with some plan that depended on Cleopatra being a little nursery kitten. Now that Cleopatra is a Queen, the plan is upset.

POTHINUS [*bowing his head submissively*] It is so.

CLEOPATRA [*exultant*] Aha!

POTHINUS [*raising his eyes keenly to hers*] Is Cleopatra then indeed a Queen, and no longer Cæsar's prisoner and slave?

CLEOPATRA. Pothinus: we are all Cæsar's slaves—all we in this land of Egypt—whether we will or no. And she who is wise enough to know this will reign when Cæsar departs.

POTHINUS. You harp on Cæsar's departure.

CLEOPATRA. What if I do?

POTHINUS. Does he not love you?

CLEOPATRA. Love me! Pothinus: Cæsar loves no one. Who are those we love. Only those whom we do not hate: all people are strangers and enemies to us except those we love. But it is not so with Cæsar. He has no hatred in him: he makes friends with everyone as he does with dogs and children. His kindness to me is a wonder: neither mother, father, nor nurse have ever taken so much care for me, or thrown open their thoughts to me so freely.

POTHINUS. Well: is not this love?

CLEOPATRA. What! when he will do as much for the first girl he meets on his way back to Rome? Ask his slave, Britannus: he has been just as good to him. Nay, ask his very horse! His kindness is not for anything in me: it is in his own nature.

POTHINUS. But how can you be sure that he does not love you as men love women?

CLEOPATRA. Because I cannot make him jealous. I have tried.

POTHINUS. Hm! Perhaps I should have asked, then, do you love him?

CLEOPATRA. Can one love a god? Besides, I love another Roman: one whom I saw long before Cæsar—no god, but a man—one who can love and hate—one whom I can hurt and who would hurt me.

POTHINUS. Does Cæsar know this?

CLEOPATRA. Yes.

POTHINUS. And he is not angry?

CLEOPATRA. He promises to send him to Egypt to please me!

POTHINUS. I do not understand this man.

CLEOPATRA [with superb contempt] You understand Cæsar! How could you? [Proudly] I do—by instinct.

POTHINUS [deferentially, after a moment's thought] Your Majesty caused me to be admitted today. What message has the Queen for me?

CLEOPATRA. This. You think that by making my brother king, you will rule in Egypt because you are his guardian and he is a little silly.

POTHINUS. The Queen is pleased to say so.

CLEOPATRA. The Queen is pleased to say this also. That Cæsar will eat up you, and Achillas, and my brother, as a cat eats up mice; and that he will put on this land of Egypt as a shepherd puts on his garment. And when he has done that, he will return to Rome, and leave Cleopatra here as his viceroy.

POTHINUS [breaking out wrathfully] That he shall never do. We have a thousand men to his ten; and we will drive him and his beggarly legions into the sea.

CLEOPATRA [with scorn, getting up to go] You rant like any common fellow. Go, then, and marshal your thousands; and make haste; for Mithridates of Pergamos is at hand with reinforcements for Cæsar. Cæsar has held you at bay with two legions: we shall see what he will do with twenty.

POTHINUS. Cleopatra—

CLEOPATRA. Enough, enough: Cæsar has spoiled me for talking to weak things like you. [*She goes out. Pothinus, with a gesture of rage, is following, when Ftatateeta enters and stops him.*]

POTHINUS. Let me go forth from this hateful place.

FTATATEETA. What angers you?

POTHINUS. The curse of all the gods of Egypt be upon her! She sold her country to the Roman, that she may buy it back from him with her kisses.

FTATATEETA. Fool: did she not tell you that she would have Cæsar gone?

POTHINUS. You listened?

FTATATEETA. I took care that some honest woman should be at hand whilst you were with her.

POTHINUS. Now by the gods—

FTATATEETA. Enough of your gods! Cæsar's gods are all powerful here. It is no use you coming to Cleopatra: you are only an Egyptian. She will not listen to any of her own race: she treats us all as children.

POTHINUS. May she perish for it!

FTATATEETA [*balefully*] May your tongue wither for that wish! Go! send for Lucius Septimius, the slayer of Pompey. He is a Roman: may be she will listen to him. Begone!

POTHINUS [*darkly*] I know to whom I must go now.

FTATATEETA [*suspiciously*] To whom, then?

POTHINUS. To a greater Roman than Lucius. And mark this, mistress. You thought, before Cæsar came, that Egypt should presently be ruled by you and your crew in the name of Cleopatra. I set myself against it—

FTATATEETA [*interrupting him—wrangling*] Ay; that it might be ruled by you and your crew in the name of Ptolemy.

POTHINUS. Better me, or even you, than a woman with a Roman heart; and that is what Cleopatra is now become.

Whilst I live, she shall never rule. So guide yourself accordingly. [*He goes out*].

It is by this time drawing on to dinner time. The table is laid on the roof of the palace; and thither Rufio is now climbing, ushered by a majestic palace official, wand of office in hand, and followed by a slave carrying an inlaid stool. After many stairs they emerge at last into a massive colonnade on the roof. Light curtains are drawn between the columns on the north and east to soften the westering sun. The official leads Rufio to one of these shaded sections. A cord for pulling the curtains apart hangs down between the pillars.

THE OFFICIAL [*bowing*] The Roman commander will await Cæsar here.

The slave sets down the stool near the southernmost column, and slips out through the curtains.

RUFIO [*sitting down, a little blown*] Pouf! That was a climb. How high have we come?

THE OFFICIAL. We are on the palace roof, O Beloved of Victory!

RUFIO. Good! the Beloved of Victory has no more stairs to get up.

A second official enters from the opposite end, walking backwards.

THE SECOND OFFICIAL. Cæsar approaches.

Cæsar, fresh from the bath, clad in a new tunic of purple silk, comes in, beaming and festive, followed by two slaves carrying a light couch, which is hardly more than an elaborately designed bench. They place it near the northmost of the two curtained columns. When this is done they slip out through the curtains; and the two officials, formally bowing, follow them. Rufio rises to receive Cæsar.

CÆSAR [*coming over to him*] Why, Rufio! [*Surveying his dress with an air of admiring astonishment*] A new baldrick! A new golden pommel to your sword! And you have had your hair cut! But not your beard—? impossible! [*He sniffs* t *Rufio's beard*]. Yes, perfumed, by Jupiter Olympus!

RUFIO [*growling*] Well: is it to please myself?

CÆSAR [*affectionately*] No, my son Rufio, but to please me —to celebrate my birthday.

RUFIO [*contemptuously*] Your birthday! You always have birthday when there is a pretty girl to be flattered or an mbassador to be conciliated. We had seven of them in ten nonths last year.

CÆSAR [*contritely*] It is true, Rufio! I shall never break my-elf of these petty deceits.

RUFIO. Who is to dine with us—besides Cleopatra?

CÆSAR. Apollodorus the Sicilian.

RUFIO. That popinjay!

CÆSAR. Come! the popinjay is an amusing dog—tells a tory; sings a song; and saves us the trouble of flattering the Queen. What does she care for old politicians and camp-fed ears like us? No, Apollodorus is good company, Rufio, ;ood company.

RUFIO. Well, he can swim a bit and fence a bit: he might e worse, if he only knew how to hold his tongue.

CÆSAR. The gods forbid he should ever learn! Oh, this nilitary life! this tedious, brutal life of action! That is the vorst of us Romans: we are mere doers and drudgers: a warm of bees turned into men. Give me a good talker— ne with wit and imagination enough to live without con- inually doing something!

RUFIO. Ay! a nice time he would have of it with you when linner was over! Have you noticed that I am before my ime?

CÆSAR. Aha! I thought that meant something. What is it?

RUFIO. Can we be overheard here?

CÆSAR. Our privacy invites eavesdropping. I can remedy hat. [*He claps his hands twice. The curtains are drawn, re- ealing the roof garden with a banqueting table set across n the middle for four persons, one at each end, and two ide by side. The side next Cæsar and Rufio is blocked with golden wine vessels and basins. A gorgeous major-domo is superintending the laying of the table by a staff of slaves. The colonnade goes round the garden at both sides to the further end, where a gap in it, like a great gateway, leaves the view open to the sky beyond the western edge of the roof, except in the middle, where a life size image of Ra, seated on a huge plinth, towers up, with hawk head and crown of asp and disk. His altar, which stands at his feet, is a single white stone.]* Now everybody can see us, nobody will think of listening to us. [*He sits down on the bench left by the two slaves*].

RUFIO [*sitting down on his stool*] Pothinus wants to speak to you. I advise you to see him: there is some plotting going on here among the women.

CÆSAR. Who is Pothinus?

RUFIO. The fellow with hair like squirrel's fur—the little King's bear leader, whom you kept prisoner.

CÆSAR [*annoyed*] And has he not escaped?

RUFIO. No.

CÆSAR [*rising imperiously*] Why not? You have been guarding this man instead of watching the enemy. Have I not told you always to let prisoners escape unless there are special orders to the contrary? Are there not enough mouths to be fed without him?

RUFIO. Yes; and if you would have a little sense and let me cut his throat, you would save his rations. Anyhow he wont escape. Three sentries have told him they would put a pilum through him if they saw him again. What more can they do? He prefers to stay and spy on us. So would I if I had to do with generals subject to fits of clemency.

CÆSAR [*resuming his seat, argued down*] Hm! And so he wants to see me.

RUFIO. Ay. I have brought him with me. He is waiting there [*jerking his thumb over his shoulder*] under guard.

CÆSAR. And you want me to see him?

RUFIO [*obstinately*] I dont want anything. I daresay you

will do what you like. Dont put it on to me.

CÆSAR [*with an air of doing it expressly to indulge Rufio*] Well, well: let us have him.

RUFIO [*calling*] Ho there, guard! Release your man and send him up. [*Beckoning*]. Come along!

Pothinus enters and stops mistrustfully between the two, looking from one to the other.

CÆSAR [*graciously*] Ah, Pothinus! You are welcome. And what is the news this afternoon?

POTHINUS. Cæsar: I come to warn you of a danger, and to make you an offer.

CÆSAR. Never mind the danger. Make the offer.

RUFIO. Never mind the offer. Whats the danger?

POTHINUS. Cæsar: you think that Cleopatra is devoted to you.

CÆSAR [*gravely*] My friend: I already know what I think. Come to your offer.

POTHINUS. I will deal plainly. I know not by what strange gods you have been enabled to defend a palace and a few yards of beach against a city and an army. Since we cut you off from Lake Mareotis, and you dug wells in the salt sea sand and brought up buckets of fresh water from them, we have known that your gods are irresistible, and that you are a worker of miracles. I no longer threaten you—

RUFIO [*sarcastically*] Very handsome of you, indeed.

POTHINUS. So be it: you are the master. Our gods sent the north west winds to keep you in our hands; but you have been too strong for them.

CÆSAR [*gently urging him to come to the point*] Yes, yes, my friend. But what then?

RUFIO. Spit it out, man. What have you to say?

POTHINUS. I have to say that you have a traitress in your camp. Cleopatra—

THE MAJOR-DOMO [*at the table, announcing*] The Queen! [*Cæsar and Rufio rise*].

RUFIO [*aside to Pothinus*] You should have spat it out

sooner, you fool. Now it is too late.

Cleopatra, in gorgeous raiment, enters in state through the gap in the colonnade, and comes down past the image of Ra and past the table to Cæsar. Her retinue, headed by Ftatateeta, joins the staff at the table. Cæsar gives Cleopatra his seat, which she takes.

CLEOPATRA [*quickly, seeing Pothinus*] What is he doing here?

CÆSAR [*seating himself beside her, in the most amiable of tempers*] Just going to tell me something about you. You shall hear it. Proceed, Pothinus.

POTHINUS [*disconcerted*] Cæsar—[*he stammers*]

CÆSAR. Well, out with it.

POTHINUS. What I have to say is for your ear, not for the Queen's.

CLEOPATRA [*with subdued ferocity*] There are means of making you speak. Take care.

POTHINUS [*defiantly*] Cæsar does not employ those means.

CÆSAR. My friend: when a man has anything to tell in this world, the difficulty is not to make him tell it, but to prevent him from telling it too often. Let me celebrate my birthday by setting you free. Farewell: we shall not meet again.

CLEOPATRA [*angrily*] Cæsar: this mercy is foolish.

POTHINUS [*to Cæsar*] Will you not give me a private audience? Your life may depend on it. [*Cæsar rises loftily*].

RUFIO [*aside to Pothinus*] Ass! Now we shall have some heroics.

CÆSAR [*oratorically*] Pothinus—

RUFIO [*interrupting him*] Cæsar: the dinner will spoil if you begin preaching your favorite sermon about life and death.

CLEOPATRA [*priggishly*] Peace, Rufio. I desire to hear Cæsar.

RUFIO [*bluntly*] Your Majesty has heard it before. You repeated it to Apollodorus last week; and he thought it was all your own. [*Cæsar's dignity collapses. Much tickled, he sits down again and looks roguishly at Cleopatra, who is furious. Rufio calls as before*] Ho there, guard! Pass the prisoner out. He is released. [*To Pothinus*] Now off with you. You have lost your chance.

POTHINUS [*his temper overcoming his prudence*] I will speak.

CÆSAR [*to Cleopatra*] You see. Torture would not have wrung a word from him.

POTHINUS. Cæsar: you have taught Cleopatra the arts by which the Romans govern the world.

CÆSAR. Alas! they cannot even govern themselves. What then?

POTHINUS. What then? Are you so besotted with her beauty that you do not see that she is impatient to reign in Egypt alone, and that her heart is set on your departure?

CLEOPATRA [*rising*] Liar!

CÆSAR [*shocked*] What! Protestations! Contradictions!

CLEOPATRA [*ashamed, but trembling with suppressed rage*] No. I do not deign to contradict. Let him talk. [*She sits down again*].

POTHINUS. From her own lips I have heard it. You are to be her catspaw: you are to tear the crown from her brother's head and set it on her own, delivering us all into her hand—delivering yourself also. And then Cæsar can return to Rome, or depart through the gate of death, which is nearer and surer.

CÆSAR [*calmly*] Well, my friend; and is not this very natural?

POTHINUS [*astonished*] Natural! Then you do not resent treachery?

CÆSAR. Resent! O thou foolish Egyptian, what have I to do with resentment? Do I resent the wind when it chills me, or the night when it makes me stumble in darkness? Shall I resent youth when it turns from age, and ambition when it

turns from servitude? To tell me such a story as this is but
to tell me that the sun will rise tomorrow.

CLEOPATRA [*unable to contain herself*] But it is false—
false. I swear it.

CÆSAR. It is true, though you swore it a thousand times,
and believed all you swore. [*She is convulsed with emotion.
To screen her, he rises and takes Pothinus to Rufio, saying*]
Come, Rufio: let us see Pothinus past the guard. I have a
word to say to him. [*Aside to them*] We must give the
Queen a moment to recover herself. [*Aloud*] Come. [*He
takes Pothinus and Rufio out with him, conversing with
them meanwhile*]. Tell your friends, Pothinus, that they
must not think I am opposed to a reasonable settlement of
the country's affairs—[*They pass out of hearing*].

CLEOPATRA [*in a stifled whisper*] Ftatateeta, Ftatateeta.

FTATATEETA [*hurrying to her from the table and petting
her*] Peace, child: be comforted—

CLEOPATRA [*interrupting her*] Can they hear us?

FTATATEETA. No, dear heart, no.

CLEOPATRA. Listen to me. If he leaves the Palace alive,
never see my face again.

FTATATEETA. He? Poth—

CLEOPATRA [*striking her on the mouth*] Strike his life out
as I strike his name from your lips. Dash him down from
the wall. Break him on the stones. Kill, kill, kill him.

FTATATEETA [*shewing all her teeth*] The dog shall perish.

CLEOPATRA. Fail in this, and you go out from before me
for ever.

FTATATEETA [*resolutely*] So be it. You shall not see my
face until his eyes are darkened.

*Cæsar comes back, with Apollodorus, exquisitely dressed,
and Rufio.*

CLEOPATRA [*to Ftatateeta*] Come soon—soon. [*Ftatateeta
turns her meaning eyes for a moment on her mistress; then
goes grimly away past Ra and out. Cleopatra runs like a
gazelle to Cæsar*] So you have come back to me, Cæsar.

[*Caressingly*] I thought you were angry. Welcome, Apollodorus. [*She gives him her hand to kiss, with her other arm about Cæsar*].

APOLLODORUS. Cleopatra grows more womanly beautiful from week to week.

CLEOPATRA. Truth, Apollodorus?

APOLLODORUS. Far, far short of the truth! Friend Rufio threw a pearl into the sea: Cæsar fished up a diamond.

CÆSAR. Cæsar fished up a touch of rheumatism, my friend. Come: to dinner! to dinner! [*They move towards the table*].

CLEOPATRA [*skipping like a young fawn*] Yes, to dinner. I have ordered such a dinner for you, Cæsar!

CÆSAR. Ay? What are we to have?

CLEOPATRA. Peacocks' brains.

CÆSAR [*as if his mouth watered*] Peacocks' brains, Apollodorus!

APOLLODORUS. Not for me. I prefer nightingales' tongues. [*He goes to one of the two covers set side by side*].

CLEOPATRA. Roast boar, Rufio!

RUFIO [*gluttonously*] Good! [*He goes to the seat next Apollodorus, on his left*].

CÆSAR [*looking at his seat, which is at the end of the table, to Ra's left hand*] What has become of my leathern cushion?

CLEOPATRA [*at the opposite end*] I have got new ones for you.

THE MAJOR-DOMO. These cushions, Cæsar, are of Maltese gauze, stuffed with rose leaves.

CÆSAR. Rose leaves! Am I a caterpillar? [*He throws the cushions away and seats himself on the leather mattress underneath*].

CLEOPATRA. What a shame! My new cushions!

THE MAJOR-DOMO [*at Cæsar's elbow*] What shall we serve to whet Cæsar's appetite?

CÆSAR. What have you got?

THE MAJOR-DOMO. Sea hedgehogs, black and white sea acorns, sea nettles, beccaficoes, purple shellfish—

CÆSAR. Any oysters?

THE MAJOR-DOMO. Assuredly.

CÆSAR. British oysters?

THE MAJOR-DOMO [*assenting*] British oysters, Cæsar.

CÆSAR. Oysters, then. [*The Major-Domo signs to a slave at each order; and the slave goes out to execute it*]. I have been in Britain—that western land of romance—the last piece of earth on the edge of the ocean that surrounds the world. I went there in search of its famous pearls. The British pearl was a fable; but in searching for it I found the British oyster.

APOLLODORUS. All posterity will bless you for it. [*To the Major-Domo*] Sea hedgehogs for me.

RUFIO. Is there nothing solid to begin with?

THE MAJOR-DOMO. Fieldfares with asparagus—

CLEOPATRA [*interrupting*] Fattened fowls! have some fattened fowls, Rufio.

RUFIO. Ay, that will do.

CLEOPATRA [*greedily*] Fieldfares for me.

THE MAJOR-DOMO. Cæsar will deign to choose his wine? Sicilian, Lesbian, Chian—

RUFIO [*contemptuously*] All Greek.

APOLLODORUS. Who would drink Roman wine when he could get Greek. Try the Lesbian, Cæsar.

CÆSAR. Bring me my barley water.

RUFIO [*with intense disgust*] Ugh! Bring me my Falernian. [*The Falernian is presently brought to him*].

CLEOPATRA [*pouting*] It is waste of time giving you dinners, Cæsar. My scullions would not condescend to your diet.

CÆSAR [*relenting*] Well, well: let us try the Lesbian. [*The Major-Domo fills Cæsar's goblet; then Cleopatra's and Apollodorus's*]. But when I return to Rome, I will make laws against these extravagances. I will even get the laws carried out.

CLEOPATRA [*coaxingly*] Never mind. Today you are to be like other people: idle, luxurious, and kind. [*She stretches *her hand to him along the table*].

CÆSAR. Well, for once I will sacrifice my comfort—[*kissing her hand*] there! [*He takes a draught of wine*]. Now are you satisfied?

CLEOPATRA. And you no longer believe that I long for your departure for Rome?

CÆSAR. I no longer believe anything. My brains are asleep. Besides, who knows whether I shall return to Rome?

RUFIO [*alarmed*] How? Eh? What?

CÆSAR. What has Rome to shew me that I have not seen already? One year of Rome is like another, except that I grow older, whilst the crowd in the Appian Way is always the same age.

APOLLODORUS. It is no better here in Egypt. The old men, when they are tired of life, say "We have seen everything except the source of the Nile."

CÆSAR [*his imagination catching fire*] And why not see that? Cleopatra: will you come with me and track the flood to its cradle in the heart of the regions of mystery? Shall we leave Rome behind us—Rome, that has achieved greatness only to learn how greatness destroys nations of men who are not great! Shall I make you a new kingdom, and build you a holy city there in the great unknown?

CLEOPATRA [*rapturously*] Yes, yes. You shall.

RUFIO. Ay: now he will conquer Africa with two legions before we come to the roast boar.

APOLLODORUS. Come: no scoffing. This is a noble scheme: in it Cæsar is no longer merely the conquering soldier, but the creative poet-artist. Let us name the holy city, and consecrate it with Lesbian wine.

CÆSAR. Cleopatra shall name it herself.

CLEOPATRA. It shall be called Cæsar's Gift to his Beloved.

APOLLODORUS. No, no. Something vaster than that—something universal, like the starry firmament.

CÆSAR [*prosaically*] Why not simply The Cradle of the Nile?

CLEOPATRA. No: the Nile is my ancestor; and he is a god. Oh! I have thought of something. The Nile shall name it himself. Let us call upon him. [*To the Major-Domo*] Send for him. [*The three men stare at one another; but the Major-Domo goes out as if he had received the most matter-of-fact order*]. And [*to the retinue*] away with you all.

The retinue withdraws, making obeisance.

A priest enters, carrying a miniature sphinx with a tiny tripod before it. A morsel of incense is smoking in the tripod. The priest comes to the table and places the image in the middle of it. The light begins to change to the magenta purple of the Egyptian sunset, as if the god had brought a strange colored shadow with him. The three men are determined not to be impressed; but they feel curious in spite of themselves.

CÆSAR. What hocus-pocus is this?

CLEOPATRA. You shall see. And it is not hocus-pocus. To do it properly, we should kill something to please him; but perhaps he will answer Cæsar without that if we spill some wine to him.

APOLLODORUS [*turning his head to look up over his shoulder at Ra*] Why not appeal to our hawkheaded friend here?

CLEOPATRA [*nervously*] Sh! He will hear you and be angry.

RUFIO [*phlegmatically*] The source of the Nile is out of his district, I expect.

CLEOPATRA. No: I will have my city named by nobody but my dear little sphinx, because it was in its arms that Cæsar found me asleep. [*She languishes at Cæsar then turns curtly to the priest*]. Go. I am a priestess, and have power to take your charge from you. [*The priest makes a reverence and goes out*]. Now let us call on the Nile all together. Perhaps he will rap on the table.

CÆSAR. What! table rapping! Are such superstitions still believed in this year 707 of the Republic?

CLEOPATRA. It is no superstition: our priests learn lots of

things from the tables. Is it not so, Apollodorus?

APOLLODORUS. Yes: I profess myself a converted man. When Cleopatra is priestess, Apollodorus is a devotee. Propose the conjuration.

CLEOPATRA. You must say with me "Send us thy voice, Father Nile."

ALL FOUR [*holding their glasses together before the idol*] Send us thy voice, Father Nile.

The death cry of a man in mortal terror and agony answers them. Appalled, the men set down their glasses, and listen. Silence. The purple deepens in the sky. Cæsar, glancing at Cleopatra, catches her pouring out her wine before the god, with gleaming eyes, and mute assurances of gratitude and worship. Apollodorus springs up and runs to the edge of the roof to peer down and listen.

CÆSAR [*looking piercingly at Cleopatra*] What was that?

CLEOPATRA [*petulantly*] Nothing. They are beating some slave.

CÆSAR. Nothing.

RUFIO. A man with a knife in him, I'll swear.

CÆSAR [*rising*] A murder!

APOLLODORUS [*at the back, waving his hand for silence*] S-sh! Silence. Did you hear that?

CÆSAR. Another cry?

APOLLODORUS [*returning to the table*] No, a thud. Something fell on the beach, I think.

RUFIO [*grimly, as he rises*] Something with bones in it, eh?

CÆSAR [*shuddering*] Hush, hush, Rufio. [*He leaves the table and returns to the colonnade: Rufio following at his left elbow, and Apollodorus at the other side*].

CLEOPATRA [*still in her place at the table*] Will you leave me, Cæsar? Apollodorus: are you going?

APOLLODORUS. Faith, dearest Queen, my appetite is gone.

CÆSAR. Go down to the courtyard, Apollodorus; and find out what has happened.

Apollodorus nods and goes out, making for the staircase

by which Rufio ascended.

CLEOPATRA. Your soldiers have killed somebody, perhaps. What does it matter?

The murmur of a crowd rises from the beach below. Cæsar and Rufio look at one another.

CÆSAR. This must be seen to. [*He is about to follow Apollodorus when Rufio stops him with a hand on his arm as Ftatateeta comes back by the far end of the roof, with dragging steps, a drowsy satiety in her eyes and in the corners of the bloodhound lips. For a moment Cæsar suspects that she is drunk with wine. Not so Rufio: he knows well the red vintage that has inebriated her*].

RUFIO [*in a low tone*] There is some mischief between these two.

FTATATEETA. The Queen looks again on the face of her servant.

Cleopatra looks at her for a moment with an exultant reflection of her murderous expression. Then she flings her arms round her; kisses her repeatedly and savagely; and tears off her jewels and heaps them on her. The two men turn from the spectacle to look at one another. Ftatateeta drags herself sleepily to the altar; kneels before Ra; and remains there in prayer. Cæsar goes to Cleopatra, leaving Rufio in the colonnade.

CÆSAR [*with searching earnestness*] Cleopatra: what has happened?

CLEOPATRA [*in mortal dread of him, but with her utmost cajolery*] Nothing, dearest Cæsar. [*With sickly sweetness, her voice almost failing*] Nothing. I am innocent. [*She approaches him affectionately*] Dear Cæsar: are you angry with me? Why do you look at me so? I have been here with you all the time. How can I know what has happened?

CÆSAR [*reflectively*] That is true.

CLEOPATRA [*greatly relieved, trying to caress him*] Of course it is true. [*He does not respond to the caress*] You know it is true, Rufio.

The murmur without suddenly swells to a roar and subsides.

RUFIO. I shall know presently. [*He makes for the altar in the burly trot that serves him for a stride, and touches Ftatateeta on the shoulder*]. Now, mistress: I shall want you. [*He orders her, with a gesture, to go before him*].

FTATATEETA [*rising and glowering at him*] My place is with the Queen.

CLEOPATRA. She has done no harm, Rufio.

CÆSAR [*to Rufio*] Let her stay.

RUFIO [*sitting down on the altar*] Very well. Then my place is here too; and you can see what is the matter for yourself. The city is in a pretty uproar, it seems.

CÆSAR [*with grave displeasure*] Rufio: there is a time for obedience.

RUFIO. And there is a time for obstinacy. [*He folds his arms doggedly*].

CÆSAR [*to Cleopatra*] Send her away.

CLEOPATRA [*whining in her eagerness to propitiate him*] Yes, I will. I will do whatever you ask me, Cæsar, always, because I love you. Ftatateeta: go away.

FTATATEETA. The Queen's word is my will. I shall be at hand for the Queen's call. [*She goes out past Ra, as she came*].

RUFIO [*following her*] Remember, Cæsar, your bodyguard is also within call. [*He follows her out*].

Cleopatra, presuming upon Cæsar's submission to Rufio, leaves the table and sits down on the bench in the colonnade.

CLEOPATRA. Why do you allow Rufio to treat you so? You should teach him his place.

CÆSAR. Teach him to be my enemy, and to hide his thoughts from me as you are now hiding yours?

CLEOPATRA [*her fears returning*] Why do you say that, Cæsar? Indeed, indeed, I am not hiding anything. You are wrong to treat me like this. [*She stifles a sob*]. I am only a child; and you turn into stone because you think some one has been killed. I cannot bear it. [*She purposely breaks down and weeps. He looks at her with profound sadness and complete coldness. She looks up to see what effect she is producing. Seeing that he is unmoved, she sits up, pretending to struggle with her emotion and to put it bravely away*]. But there: I know you hate tears: you shall not be troubled with them. I know you are not angry, but only sad; only I am so silly, I cannot help being hurt when you speak coldly. Of course you are quite right: it is dreadful to think of anyone being killed or even hurt; and I hope nothing really serious has—[*her voice dies away under his contemptuous penetration*].

CÆSAR. What has frightened you into this? What have you done? [*A trumpet sounds on the beach below*]. Aha! that sounds like the answer.

CLEOPATRA [*sinking back trembling on the bench and covering her face with her hands*] I have not betrayed you, Cæsar: I swear it.

CÆSAR. I know that. I have not trusted you. [*He turns from her, and is about to go out when Apollodorus and Britannus drag in Lucius Septimius to him. Rufio follows. Cæsar shudders*]. Again, Pompey's murderer!

RUFIO. The town has gone mad, I think. They are for tearing the palace down and driving us into the sea straight away. We laid hold of this renegade in clearing them out of the courtyard.

CÆSAR. Release him. [*They let go his arms*]. What has offended the citizens, Lucius Septimius?

LUCIUS. What did you expect, Cæsar? Pothinus was a favorite of theirs.

CÆSAR. What has happened to Pothinus? I set him free, here, not half an hour ago. Did they not pass him out?

LUCIUS. Ay, through the gallery arch sixty feet above ground, with three inches of steel in his ribs. He is as dead as Pompey. We are quits now, as to killing—you and I.

CÆSAR [*shocked*] Assassinated!—our prisoner, our guest!

[*He turns reproachfully on Rufio*] Rufio—

RUFIO [*emphatically—anticipating the question*] Whoever did it was a wise man and a friend of yours [*Cleopatra is greatly emboldened*]; but none of us had a hand in it. So it is no use to frown at me. [*Cæsar turns and looks at Cleopatra*].

CLEOPATRA [*violently—rising*] He was slain by order of the Queen of Egypt. I am not Julius Cæsar the dreamer, who allows every slave to insult him. Rufio has said I did well: now the others shall judge me too. [*She turns to the others*]. This Pothinus sought to make me conspire with him to betray Cæsar to Achillas and Ptolemy. I refused; and he cursed me and came privily to Cæsar to accuse me of his own treachery. I caught him in the act; and he insulted me—me, the Queen! to my face. Cæsar would not avenge me: he spoke him fair and set him free. Was I right to avenge myself? Speak, Lucius.

LUCIUS. I do not gainsay it. But you will get little thanks from Cæsar for it.

CLEOPATRA. Speak, Apollodorus. Was I wrong?

APOLLODORUS. I have only one word of blame, most beautiful. You should have called upon me, your knight; and in a fair duel I should have slain the slanderer.

CLEOPATRA [*passionately*] I will be judged by your very slave, Cæsar. Britannus: speak. Was I wrong?

BRITANNUS. Were treachery, falsehood, and disloyalty left unpunished, society must become like an arena full of wild beasts, tearing one another to pieces. Cæsar is in the wrong.

CÆSAR [*with quiet bitterness*] And so the verdict is against me, it seems.

CLEOPATRA [*vehemently*] Listen to me, Cæsar. If one man in all Alexandria can be found to say that I did wrong, I swear to have myself crucified on the door of the palace by my own slaves.

CÆSAR. If one man in all the world can be found, now or forever, to know that you did wrong, that man will have either to conquer the world as I have, or be crucified by it [*The uproar in the streets again reaches them*]. Do you hear? These knockers at your gate are also believers in vengeance and in stabbing. You have slain their leader: it is right that they shall slay you. If you doubt it, ask your four counsellors here. And then in the name of that right [*he emphasizes the word with great scorn*] shall I not slay them for murdering their Queen, and be slain in my turn by their countrymen as the invader of their fatherland? Can Rome do less then than slay these slayers, too, to shew the world how Rome avenges her sons and her honor. And so, to the end of history, murder shall breed murder, always in the name of right and honor and peace, until the gods are tired of blood and create a race that can understand. [*Fierce uproar. Cleopatra becomes white with terror*]. Hearken, you who must not be insulted. Go near enough to catch their words: you will find them bitterer than the tongue of Pothinus. [*Loftily, wrapping himself up in an impenetrable dignity*] Let the Queen of Egypt now give her orders for vengeance, and take her measures for defence; for she has renounced Cæsar. [*He turns to go*].

CLEOPATRA [*terrified, running to him and falling on her knees*] You will not desert me, Cæsar. You will defend the palace.

CÆSAR. You have taken the powers of life and death upon you. I am only a dreamer.

CLEOPATRA. But they will kill me.

CÆSAR. And why not?

CLEOPATRA. In pity—

CÆSAR. Pity! What! has it come to this so suddenly, that nothing can save you now but pity? Did it save Pothinus?

She rises, wringing her hands, and goes back to the bench in despair. Apollodorus shews his sympathy with her by quietly posting himself behind the bench. The sky has by this time become the most vivid purple, and soon begins to change to a glowing pale orange, against which the colon-

nade and the great image shew darklier and darklier.

RUFIO. Cæsar: enough of preaching. The enemy is at the gate.

CÆSAR [*turning on him and giving way to his wrath*] Ay; and what has held him baffled at the gate all these months? Was it my folly, as you deem it, or your wisdom? In this Egyptian Red Sea of blood, whose hand has held all your heads above the waves? [*Turning on Cleopatra*] And yet, when Cæsar says to such an one, "Friend, go free," you, clinging for your little life to my sword, dare steal out and stab him in the back? And you, soldiers and gentlemen, and honest servants as you forget that you are, applaud this assassination, and say "Cæsar is in the wrong." By the gods, I am tempted to open my hand and let you all sink into the flood.

CLEOPATRA [*with a ray of cunning hope*] But, Cæsar, if you do, you will perish yourself.

Cæsar's eyes blaze.

RUFIO [*greatly alarmed*] Now, by great Jove, you filthy little Egyptian rat, that is the very word to make him walk out alone into the city and leave us here to be cut to pieces. [*Desperately, to Cæsar*] Will you desert us because we are a parcel of fools? I mean no harm by killing: I do it as a cat, by instinct. We are all dogs at your heels; but we have served you faithfully.

CÆSAR [*relenting*] Alas, Rufio, my son, my son: as dogs we' are like to perish now in the streets.

APOLLODORUS [*at his post behind Cleopatra's seat*] Cæsar: what you say has an Olympian ring in it: it must be right; for it is fine art. But I am still on the side of Cleopatra. If we must die, she shall not want the devotion of a man's heart nor the strength of a man's arm.

CLEOPATRA [*sobbing*] But I dont want to die.

CÆSAR [*sadly*] Oh, ignoble, ignoble!

LUCIUS [*coming forward between Cæsar and Cleopatra*] Hearken to me, Cæsar. It may be ignoble; but I also mean to live as long as I can.

CÆSAR. Well, my friend, you are likely to outlive Cæsar. Is it any magic of mine, think you, that has kept your army and this whole city at bay for so long? Yesterday, what quarrel had they with me that they should risk their lives against me? But today we have flung them down their hero, murdered; and now every man of them is set upon clearing out this nest of assassins—for such we are and no more. Take courage then; and sharpen your sword. Pompey's head has fallen; and Cæsar's head is ripe.

APOLLODORUS. Does Cæsar despair?

CÆSAR [*with infinite pride*] He who has never hoped can never despair. Cæsar, in good or bad fortune, looks his fate in the face.

LUCIUS. Look it in the face, then; and it will smile as it always has on Cæsar.

CÆSAR [*with involuntary haughtiness*] Do you presume to encourage me?

LUCIUS. I offer you my services. I will change sides if you will have me.

CÆSAR [*suddenly coming down to earth again, and looking sharply at him, divining that there is something behind the offer*] What! At this point?

LUCIUS [*firmly*] At this point.

RUFIO. Do you suppose Cæsar is mad, to trust you?

LUCIUS. I do not ask him to trust me until he is victorious. I ask for my life, and for a command in Cæsar's army. And since Cæsar is a fair dealer, I will pay in advance.

CÆSAR. Pay! How?

LUCIUS. With a piece of good news for you.

Cæsar divines the news in a flash.

RUFIO. What news?

CÆSAR [*with an elate and buoyant energy which makes Cleopatra sit up and stare*] What news! What news, did you say, my son Rufio? The relief has arrived: what other news remains for us? Is it not so, Lucius Septimius? Mithridates of Pergamos is on the march.

LUCIUS. He has taken Pelusium.

CÆSAR [*delighted*] Lucius Septimius: you are henceforth my officer. Rufio: the Egyptians must have sent every soldier from the city to prevent Mithridates crossing the Nile. There is nothing in the streets now but mob—mob!

LUCIUS. It is so. Mithridates is marching by the great road to Memphis to cross above the Delta. Achillas will fight him there.

CÆSAR [*all audacity*] Achillas shall fight Cæsar there. See, Rufio. [*He runs to the table; snatches a napkin; and draws a plan on it with his finger dipped in wine, whilst Rufio and Lucius Septimius crowd about him to watch, all looking closely, for the light is now almost gone*]. Here is the palace [*pointing to his plan*]: here is the theatre. You [*to Rufio*] take twenty men and pretend to go by that street [*pointing it out*]; and whilst they are stoning you, out go the cohorts by this and this. My streets are right, are they, Lucius?

LUCIUS. Ay, that is the fig market—

CÆSAR [*too much excited to listen to him*] I saw them the day we arrived. Good! [*He throws the napkin on the table, and comes down again into the colonnade*]. Away, Britannus: tell Petronius that within an hour half our forces must take ship for the western lake. See to my horse and armor. [*Britannus runs out*] With the rest, I shall march round the lake and up the Nile to meet Mithridates. Away, Lucius; and give the word. [*Lucius hurries out after Britannus*]. Apollodorus: lend me your sword and your right arm for this campaign.

APOLLODORUS. Ay, and my heart and life to boot.

CÆSAR [*grasping his hand*] I accept both. [*Mighty handshake*]. Are you ready for work?

APOLLODORUS. Ready for Art—the Art of War [*he rushes out after Lucius, totally forgetting Cleopatra*].

RUFIO. Come! this is something like business.

CÆSAR [*buoyantly*] Is it not, my only son? [*He claps his*

hands. The slaves hurry in to the table]. No more of this mawkish revelling: away with all this stuff: shut it out of my sight and be off with you. [*The slaves begin to remove the table; and the curtains are drawn, shutting in the colonnade*]. You understand about the streets, Rufio?

RUFIO. Ay, I think I do. I will get through them, at all events.

The bucina sounds busily in the courtyard beneath.

CÆSAR. Come, then: we must talk to the troops and hearten them. You down to the beach: I to the courtyard. [*He makes for the staircase*].

CLEOPATRA [*rising from her seat, where she has been quite neglected all this time, and stretching out her hands timidly to him*] Cæsar.

CÆSAR [*turning*] Eh?

CLEOPATRA. Have you forgotten me?

CÆSAR [*indulgently*] I am busy now, my child, busy. When I return your affairs shall be settled. Farewell; and be good and patient.

He goes, preoccupied and quite indifferent. She stands with clenched fists, in speechless rage and humiliation.

RUFIO. That game is played and lost, Cleopatra. The woman always gets the worst of it.

CLEOPATRA [*haughtily*] Go. Follow your master.

RUFIO [*in her ear, with rough familiarity*] A word first. Tell your executioner that if Pothinus had been properly killed—in the throat—he would not have called out. Your man bungled his work.

CLEOPATRA [*enigmatically*] How do you know it was a man?

RUFIO [*startled, and puzzled*] It was not you: you were with us when it happened. [*She turns her back scornfully on him. He shakes his head, and draws the curtains to go out. It is now a magnificent moonlit night. The table has been removed. Ftatateeta is seen in the light of the moon and stars, again in prayer before the white altar-stone of Ra. Rufio*

*starts; closes the curtains again softly; and says in a low voice
to Cleopatra*] Was it she? with her own hand?

CLEOPATRA [*threateningly*] Whoever it was, let my enemies
beware of her. Look to it, Rufio, you who dare make the
Queen of Egypt a fool before Cæsar.

RUFIO [*looking grimly at her*] I will look to it, Cleopatra.
[*He nods in confirmation of the promise, and slips out
through the curtains, loosening his sword in its sheath as he
goes*].

ROMAN SOLDIERS [*in the courtyard below*] Hail, Cæsar!
Hail, hail!

*Cleopatra listens. The bucina sounds again, followed by
several trumpets.*

CLEOPATRA [*wringing her hands and calling*] Ftatateeta.
Ftatateeta. It is dark; and I am alone. Come to me. [*Silence*]
Ftatateeta. [*Louder*] Ftatateeta. [*Silence. In a panic she
snatches the cord and pulls the curtains apart*].

*Ftatateeta is lying dead on the altar of Ra, with her throat
cut. Her blood deluges the white stone.*

ACT V

High noon. Festival and military pageant on the esplanade before the palace. In the east harbor Cæsar's galley, so gorgeously decorated that it seems to be rigged with flowers, is alongside the quay, close to the steps Apollodorus descended when he embarked with the carpet. A Roman guard is posted there in charge of a gangway, whence a red floorcloth is laid down the middle of the esplanade, turning off to the north opposite the central gate in the palace front, which shuts in the esplanade on the south side. The broad steps of the gate, crowded with Cleopatra's ladies, all in their gayest attire, are like a flower garden. The façade is lined by her guard, officered by the same gallants to whom Bel Affris announced the coming of Cæsar six months before in the old palace on the Syrian border. The north side is lined by Roman soldiers, with the townsfolk on tiptoe behind them, peering over their heads at the cleared esplanade, in which the officers stroll about, chatting. Among these are Belzanor and the Persian; also the centurion, vinewood cudgel in hand, battle worn, thick-booted, and much outshone, both socially and decoratively, by the Egyptian officers.

Apollodorus makes his way through the townsfolk and calls to the officers from behind the Roman line.

APOLLODORUS. Hullo! May I pass?

CENTURION. Pass Apollodorus the Sicilian there! [*The soldiers let him through*].

BELZANOR. Is Cæsar at hand?

APOLLODORUS. Not yet. He is still in the market place. I could not stand any more of the roaring of the soldiers! After half an hour of the enthusiasm of an army, one feels the need of a little sea air.

PERSIAN. Tell us the news. Hath he slain the priests?

APOLLODORUS. Not he. They met him in the market place with ashes on their heads and their gods in their hands. They placed the gods at his feet. The only one that was worth looking at was Apis: a miracle of gold and ivory work. By my advice he offered the chief priest two talents for it.

BELZANOR [*appalled*] Apis the all-knowing for two talents! What said the chief Priest?

APOLLODORUS. He invoked the mercy of Apis, and asked for five.

BELZANOR. There will be famine and tempest in the land for this.

PERSIAN. Pooh! Why did not Apis cause Cæsar to be vanquished by Achillas? Any fresh news from the war, Apollodorus?

APOLLODORUS. The little King Ptolemy was drowned.

BELZANOR. Drowned! How?

APOLLODORUS. With the rest of them. Cæsar attacked them from three sides at once and swept them into the Nile. Ptolemy's barge sank.

BELZANOR. A marvellous man, this Cæsar! Will he come soon, think you?

APOLLODORUS. He was settling the Jewish question when I left.

A flourish of trumpets from the north, and commotion among the townsfolk, announces the approach of Cæsar.

PERSIAN. He has made short work of them. Here he comes. [*He hurries to his post in front of the Egyptian lines*].

BELZANOR [*following him*] Ho there! Cæsar comes.

The soldiers stand at attention, and dress their lines. Apollodorus goes to the Egyptian line.

CENTURION [*hurrying to the gangway guard*] Attention there! Cæsar comes.

Cæsar arrives in state with Rufio: Britannus following. The soldiers receive him with enthusiastic shouting.

CÆSAR. I see my ship awaits me. The hour of Cæsar's farewell to Egypt has arrived. And now, Rufio, what remains to be done before I go?

RUFIO [*at his left hand*] You have not yet appointed a Roman governor for this province.

CÆSAR [*looking whimsically at him, but speaking with perfect gravity*] What say you to Mithridates of Pergamos, my reliever and rescuer, the great son of Eupator?

RUFIO. Why, that you will want him elsewhere. Do you forget that you have some three or four armies to conquer on your way home?

CÆSAR. Indeed! Well, what say you to yourself?

RUFIO [*incredulously*] I! I a governor! What are you dreaming of? Do you not know that I am only the son of a freedman?

CÆSAR [*affectionately*] Has not Cæsar called you his son? [*Calling to the whole assembly*] Peace awhile there; and hear me.

THE ROMAN SOLDIERS. Hear Cæsar.

CÆSAR. Hear the service, quality, rank and name of the Roman governor. By service, Cæsar's shield; by quality, Cæsar's friend; by rank, a Roman soldier. [*The Roman soldiers give a triumphant shout*]. By name, Rufio. [*They shout again*].

RUFIO [*kissing Cæsar's hand*] Ay: I am Cæsar's shield; but of what use shall I be when I am no longer on Cæsar's arm? Well, no matter—[*He becomes husky, and turns away to recover himself*].

CÆSAR. Where is that British Islander of mine?

BRITANNUS [*coming forward on Cæsar's right hand*] Here, Cæsar.

CÆSAR. Who bade you, pray, thrust yourself into the battle of the Delta, uttering the barbarous cries of your native land, and affirming yourself a match for any four of the Egyptians, to whom you applied unseemly epithets?

BRITANNUS. Cæsar: I ask you to excuse the language that escaped me in the heat of the moment.

CÆSAR. And how did you, who cannot, swim, cross the canal with us when we stormed the camp?

BRITANNUS. Cæsar: I clung to the tail of your horse.

CÆSAR. These are not the deeds of a slave, Britannicus, but of a free man.

BRITANNUS. Cæsar: I was born free.

CÆSAR. But they call you Cæsar's slave.

BRITANNUS. Only as Cæsar's slave have I found real freedom.

CÆSAR [moved] Well said. Ungrateful that I am, I was about to set you free; but now I will not part from you for a million talents. [He claps him friendly on the shoulder. Britannus, gratified, but a trifle shamefaced, takes his hand and kisses it sheepishly].

BELZANOR [to the Persian] This Roman knows how to make men serve him.

PERSIAN. Ay: men too humble to become dangerous rivals to him.

BELZANOR. O subtle one! O cynic!

CÆSAR [seeing Apollodorus in the Egyptian corner, and calling to him] Apollodorus: I leave the art of Egypt in your charge. Remember: Rome loves art and will encourage it ungrudgingly.

APOLLODORUS. I understand, Cæsar. Rome will produce no art itself; but it will buy up and take away whatever the other nations produce.

CÆSAR. What! Rome produce no art! Is peace not an art? is war not an art? is government not an art? is civilization not an art? All these we give you in exchange for a few ornaments. You will have the best of the bargain. [Turning to Rufio] And now, what else have I to do before I embark? [Trying to recollect] There is something I cannot remember: what can it be? Well, well: it must remain undone: we must not waste this favorable wind. Farewell, Rufio.

RUFIO. Cæsar: I am loth to let you go to Rome without your shield. There are too many daggers there.

CÆSAR. It matters not: I shall finish my life's work on my way back; and then I shall have lived long enough. Besides: I have always disliked the idea of dying: I had rather be killed. Farewell.

RUFIO [*with a sigh, raising his hands and giving Cæsar up as incorrigible*] Farewell. [*They shake hands*].

CÆSAR [*waving his hand to Apollodorus*] Farewell, Apollodorus, and my friends, all of you. Aboard!

The gangway is run out from the quay to the ship. As Cæsar moves towards it, Cleopatra, cold and tragic, cunningly dressed in black, without ornaments or decoration of any kind, and thus making a striking figure among the brilliantly dressed bevy of ladies as she passes through it, comes from the palace and stands on the steps. Cæsar does not see her until she speaks.

CLEOPATRA. Has Cleopatra no part in this leavetaking?

CÆSAR [*enlightened*] Ah, I knew there was something. [*To Rufio*] How could you let me forget her, Rufio? [*Hastening to her*] Had I gone without seeing you, I should never have forgiven myself. [*He takes her hands, and brings her into the middle of the esplanade. She submits stonily*]. Is this mourning for me?

CLEOPATRA. No.

CÆSAR [*remorsefully*] Ah, that was thoughtless of me! It is for your brother.

CLEOPATRA. No.

CÆSAR. For whom, then?

CLEOPATRA. Ask the Roman governor whom you have left us.

CÆSAR. Rufio?

CLEOPATRA. Yes: Rufio. [*She points at him with deadly scorn*]. He who is to rule here in Cæsar's name, in Cæsar's way, according to Cæsar's boasted laws of life.

CÆSAR [*dubiously*] He is to rule as he can, Cleopatra. He has taken the work upon him, and will do it in his own way.

CLEOPATRA. Not in your way, then?

CÆSAR [*puzzled*] What do you mean by my way?

CLEOPATRA. Without punishment. Without revenge. Without judgment.

CÆSAR [*approvingly*] Ay: that is the right way, the great way, the only possible way in the end. [*To Rufio*] Believe it, Rufio, if you can.

RUFIO. Why, I believe it, Cæsar. You have convinced me of it long ago. But look you. You are sailing for Numidia today. Now tell me: if you meet a hungry lion there, you will not punish it for wanting to eat you?

CÆSAR [*wondering what he is driving at*] No.

RUFIO. Nor revenge upon it the blood of those it has already eaten.

CÆSAR. No.

RUFIO. Nor judge it for its guiltiness.

CÆSAR. No.

RUFIO. What, then, will you do to save your life from it?

CÆSAR [*promptly*] Kill it, man, without malice, just as it would kill me. What does this parable of the lion mean?

RUFIO. Why, Cleopatra had a tigress that killed men at her bidding. I thought she might bid it kill you some day. Well, had I not been Cæsar's pupil, what pious things might I not have done to that tigress! I might have punished it. I might have revenged Pothinus on it.

CÆSAR [*interjects*] Pothinus!

RUFIO [*continuing*] I might have judged it. But I put all these follies behind me; and, without malice, only cut its throat. And that is why Cleopatra comes to you in mourning.

CLEOPATRA [*vehemently*] He has shed the blood of my servant Ftatateeta. On your head be it as upon his, Cæsar, if you hold him free of it.

CÆSAR [*energetically*] On my head be it, then; for it was well done. Rufio: had you set yourself in the seat of the judge, and with hateful ceremonies and appeals to the gods handed that woman over to some hired executioner to be slain before the people in the name of justice, never again would I have touched your hand without a shudder. But this was natural slaying: I feel no horror at it.

Rufio, satisfied, nods at Cleopatra, mutely inviting her to mark that.

CLEOPATRA [*pettish and childish in her impotence*] No: not when a Roman slays an Egyptian. All the world will now see how unjust and corrupt Cæsar is.

CÆSAR [*taking her hands coaxingly*] Come: do not be angry with me. I am sorry for that poor Totateeta. [*She laughs in spite of herself*]. Aha! you are laughing. Does that mean reconciliation?

CLEOPATRA [*angry with herself for laughing*] No, no, NO!! But it is so ridiculous to hear you call her Totateeta.

CÆSAR. What! As much a child as ever, Cleopatra! Have I not made a woman of you after all?

CLEOPATRA. Oh, it is you who are a great baby: you make me seem silly because you will not behave seriously. But you have treated me badly; and I do not forgive you.

CÆSAR. Bid me farewell.

CLEOPATRA. I will not.

CÆSAR [*coaxing*] I will send you a beautiful present from Rome.

CLEOPATRA [*proudly*] Beauty from Rome to Egypt indeed! What can Rome give me that Egypt cannot give me?

APOLLODORUS. That is true, Cæsar. If the present is to be really beautiful, I shall have to buy it for you in Alexandria.

CÆSAR. You are forgetting the treasures for which Rome is most famous, my friend. You cannot buy them in Alexandria.

APOLLODORUS. What are they, Cæsar?

CÆSAR. Her sons. Come, Cleopatra: forgive me and bid me farewell; and I will send you a man, Roman from head to heel and Roman of the noblest; not old and ripe for the knife; not lean in the arms and cold in the heart; not hiding a bald head under his conqueror's laurels; not stooped with the weight of the world on his shoulders; but brisk and fresh, strong and young, hoping in the morning, fighting in the day, and revelling in the evening. Will you take such an one in exchange for Cæsar?

CLEOPATRA [*palpitating*] His name, his name?

CÆSAR. Shall it be Mark Antony? [*She throws herself into his arms*].

RUFIO. You are a bad hand at a bargain, mistress, if you will swop Cæsar for Antony.

CÆSAR. So now you are satisfied.

CLEOPATRA. You will not forget.

CÆSAR. I will not forget. Farewell: I do not think we shall meet again. Farewell. [*He kisses her on the forehead. She is much affected and begins to sniff. He embarks*].

THE ROMAN SOLDIERS [*as he sets his foot on the gangway*] Hail, Cæsar; and farewell!

He reaches the ship and returns Rufio's wave of the hand.

APOLLODORUS [*to Cleopatra*] No tears, dearest Queen: they stab your servant to the heart. He will return some day.

CLEOPATRA. I hope not. But I cant help crying, all the same. [*She waves her handkerchief to Cæsar; and the ship begins to move*].

THE ROMAN SOLDIERS [*drawing their swords and raising them in the air*] Hail, Cæsar!

NOTES TO CÆSAR AND CLEOPATRA

CLEOPATRA'S CURE FOR BALDNESS

FOR the sake of conciseness in a hurried situation I have made Cleopatra recommend rum. This, I am afraid, is an anachronism: the only real one in the play. To balance it, I give a couple of the remedies she actually believed in. They are quoted by Galen from Cleopatra's book on Cosmetic.

"For bald patches, powder red sulphuret of arsenic and take it up with oak gum, as much as it will bear. Put on a rag and apply, having soaped the place well first. I have mixed the above with a foam of nitre, and it worked well."

Several other receipts follow, ending with: "The following is the best of all, acting for fallen hairs, when applied with oil or pomatum; acts for falling off of eyelashes or for people getting bald all over. It is wonderful. Of domestic mice burnt, one part; of vine rag burnt, one part; of horse's teeth burnt, one part; of bear's grease one; of deer's marrow one; of reed bark one. To be pounded when dry, and mixed with plenty of honey til it gets the consistency of honey; then the bear's grease and marrow to be mixed (when melted), the medicine to be put in a brass flask, and the bald part rubbed til it sprouts."

Concerning these ingredients, my fellow-dramatist Gilbert Murray, who, as a Professor of Greek, has applied to classical antiquity the methods of high scholarship (my own method is pure divination), writes to me as follows: "Some of this I dont understand, and possibly Galen did not, as he quotes your heroine's own language. Foam of nitre is, I think, something like soapsuds. Reed bark is an odd expression. It might mean the outside membrane of a reed: I do not know what it ought to be called. In the burnt mice receipt I take it that you first mixed the solid powders with honey, and then added the grease. I expect Cleopatra preferred it because in most of the others you have to lacerate the skin, prick it, or rub it till it bleeds. I do not know what vine rag is. I translate literally."

APPARENT ANACHRONISMS

The only way to write a play which shall convey to the general public an impression of antiquity is to make the characters speak blank verse and abstain from reference to steam, telegraphy, or any of the material conditions of their existence. The more ignorant men are, the more convinced are they that their little parish and their little chapel is an apex to which civilization and philosophy has painfully struggled up the pyramid of time from a desert of savagery. Savagery, they think, became barbarism; barbarism became ancient civilization; ancient civilization became Pauline Christianity; Pauline Christianity became Roman Catholicism; Roman Catholicism became the Dark Ages; and the Dark Ages were finally enlightened by the Protestant instincts of the English race. The whole process is summed up as Progress with a capital P. And any elderly gentleman of Progressive temperament will testify that the improvement since he was a boy is enormous.

Now if we count the generations of Progressive elderly gentlemen since, say, Plato, and add together the successive enormous improvements to which each of them has testified, it will strike us at once as an unaccountable fact that the world, instead of having been improved in 67 generations out of all recognition, presents, on the whole, a rather less dignified appearance in Ibsen's Enemy of the People than in Plato's Republic. And in truth, the period of time covered by history is far too short to allow of any perceptible progress in the popular sense of Evolution of the Human Species. The notion that there has been any such Progress since Cæsar's time (less than 20 centuries) is too absurd for discussion. All the savagery, barbarism, dark ages and the rest of it of which we have any record as existing in the past, exists at the present moment. A British carpenter or stonemason may point out that he gets twice as much money for his labor as his father did in the same trade, and that his suburban house, with its bath, its cottage piano, its drawing room suite, and its album of photographs, would have shamed the plainness of his grandmother's. But the descendants of feudal barons, living in squalid lodgings on a salary of fifteen shillings a week instead of in castles on princely revenues, do not congratulate the world on the change. Such changes, in fact, are not to the point. It has been known, as far back as our records go, that man running wild in the woods is different from man kennelled in a city slum; that a dog seems to understand a shepherd better than a hewer of wood and drawer of water can understand an astronomer; and that breeding, gentle nurture, and luxurious food and shelter will produce a kind of man with whom the common laborer is socially incompatible. The same thing is true of horses and dogs. Now there is clearly room for great changes in the world by increasing the percentage of individuals who are carefully bred and gently nurtured, even to finally making the most of every man and woman born. But that possibility existed in the days of the Hittites as much as it does today. It does not give the slightest real support to the common assumption that the civilized contemporaries of the Hittites were unlike their civilized descendants today.

This would appear the tritest commonplace if it were not that the ordinary citizen's ignorance of the past combines with his idealization of the present to mislead and flatter him. Our latest book on the new railway across Asia describes the dulness of the Siberian farmer and the vulgar pursepride of the Siberian man of business without the least consciousness that the string of contemptuous instances given might have been saved by writing simply "Farmers and provincial plutocrats in Siberia are exactly what they are in England."

The latest professor descanting on the civilization of the Western Empire in the fifth century feels bound to assume, in the teeth of his own researches, that the Christian was one sort of animal and the Pagan another. It might as well be assumed as indeed it generally is assumed by implication, that a murder committed with a poisoned arrow is different from a murder committed with a Mauser rifle. All such notions are illusions. Go back to the first syllable of recorded time, and there you will find your Christian and your Pagan, your yokel and your poet, helot and hero, Don Quixote and Sancho, Tamino and Papageno, Newton and bushman unable to count eleven, all alive and contemporaneous, and all convinced that they are the heirs of all the ages and the privileged recipients of THE truth (all others damnable heresies), just as you have them today, flourishing in countries each of which is the bravest and best that ever sprang at Heaven's command from out the azure main.

Again, there is the illusion of "increased command over Nature," meaning that cotton is cheap and that ten miles of country road on a bicycle have replaced four on foot. But even if man's increased command over Nature included any increased command over himself (the only sort of command relevant to his evolution into a higher being), the fact remains that it is only by running away from the increased command over Nature to country places where Nature is still in primitive command over Man that he can recover from the effects of the smoke, the stench, the foul air, the overcrowding, the racket, the ugliness, the dirt which the cheap cotton costs us. If manufacturing activity means Progress, the town must be more advanced than the country; and the field laborers and village artisans of today must be much less changed from servants of Job than the proletariat of modern London from the proletariat of Cæsar's Rome. Yet the cockney proletarian is so inferior to the village laborer that it is only by steady recruiting from the country that London is kept alive. This does not seem as if the change since Job's time were Progress in the popular sense: quite the reverse. The common stock of discoveries in physics has accumulated a little: that is all.

One more illustration. Is the Englishman prepared to admit that the American is his superior as a human being? I ask this question because the scarcity of labor in America relatively to the demand for it has led to a development of machinery there, and a consequent "increase of command over Nature" which makes many of our English methods appear almost medieval to the up-to-date Chicagoan. This means that the American has an advantage over the Englishman of exactly the same nature that the Englishman has over the contemporaries of Cicero. Is the Englishman prepared to draw the same conclusion in both cases? I think not. The American, of course, will draw it cheerfully; but I must then ask him whether, since a modern negro has a greater "command over Nature" than Washington had, we are also to accept the conclusion, involved in his former one, that humanity has progressed from Washington to the *fin de siècle* negro.

Finally, I would point out that if life is crowned by its success and devotion in industrial organization and ingenuity, we had better worship the ant and the bee (as moralists urge us to do in our childhood), and humble ourselves before the arrogance of the birds of Aristophanes.

My reason then for ignoring the popular conception of Progress in Cæsar and Cleopatra is that there is no reason to suppose that any Progress has taken place since their time. But even if I shared the popular delusion, I do not see that I could have made any essential difference in the play. I can only imitate humanity as I know it. Nobody knows whether Shakespear thought that ancient Athenian joiners, weavers, or bellows menders were any different from Elizabethan ones; but it is quite certain that he could not have made them so, unless, indeed, he had played the literary man and made Quince say, not "Is all our company here?" but "Bottom:

was not that Socrates that passed us at the Piræus with Glaucon and Polemarchus on his way to the house of Kephalus?" And so on.

CLEOPATRA

Cleopatra was only sixteen when Cæsar went to Egypt; but in Egypt sixteen is a riper age than it is in England. The childishness I have ascribed to her, as far as it is childishness of character and not lack of experience, is not a matter of years. It may be observed in our own climate at the present day in many women of fifty. It is a mistake to suppose that the difference between wisdom and folly has anything to do with the difference between physical age and physical youth. Some women are younger at seventy than most women at seventeen.

It must be borne in mind, too, that Cleopatra was a queen, and was therefore not the typical Greek-cultured, educated Egyptian lady of her time. To represent her by any such type would be as absurd as to represent George IV by a type founded on the attainments of Sir Isaac Newton. It is true that an ordinarily well educated Alexandrian girl of her time would no more have believed bogey stories about the Romans than the daughter of a modern Oxford professor would believe them about the Germans (though, by the way, it is possible to talk great nonsense at Oxford about foreigners when we are at war with them). But I do not feel bound to believe that Cleopatra was well educated. Her father, the illustrious Flute Blower, was not at all a parent of the Oxford professor type. And Cleopatra was a chip of the old block.

BRITANNUS

I find among those who have read this play in manuscript a strong conviction that an ancient Briton could not possibly have been like a modern one. I see no reason to adopt this curious view. It is true that the Roman and Norman conquests must have for a time disturbed the normal British type produced by the climate. But Britannus, born before these events, represents the unadulterated Briton who fought Cæsar and impressed Roman observers much as we should expect the ancestors of Mr Podsnap to impress the cultivated Italians of their time.

I am told that it is not scientific to treat national character as a product of climate. This only shews the wide difference between common knowledge and the intellectual game called science. We have men of exactly the same stock, and speaking the same language, growing in Great Britain, in Ireland, and in America. The result is three of the most distinctly marked nationalities under the sun. Racial characteristics are quite another matter. The difference between a Jew and a Gentile has nothing to do with the difference between an Englishman and a German. The characteristics of Britannus are local characteristics, not race characteristics. In an ancient Briton they would, I take it, be exaggerated, since modern Britain, disforested, drained, urbanified and consequently cosmopolized, is presumably less characteristically British than Cæsar's Britain.

And again I ask does anyone who, in the light of a competent knowledge of his own age, has studied history from contemporary documents, believe that 67 generations of promiscuous marriage have made any appreciable difference in the human fauna of these isles? Certainly I do not.

JULIUS CÆSAR

As to Cæsar himself, I have purposely avoided the usual anachronism of going to Cæsar's books, and concluding that the style is the man. That is only true of authors who have the specific literary genius, and have practised long enough to attain complete self-expression in letters. It is not true even on these conditions in an age when literature is conceived as a game of style, and not as a vehicle of self-expression by the author. Now Cæsar was an amateur stylist writing books of travel and campaign histories in a style so impersonal that the authenticity of the later volumes is disputed. They reveal some of his qualities just as the Voyage of a Naturalist Round the World reveals some of Darwin's, without expressing his private personality. An Englishman reading them would say that Cæsar was a man of great common sense and good taste, meaning thereby a man without originality or moral courage.

In exhibiting Cæsar as a much more various person than the historian of the Gallic wars, I hope I have not been too much imposed on by the dramatic illusion to which all great men owe part of their reputation and some the whole of it. I admit that reputations gained in war are specially questionable. Able civilians taking up the profession of arms, like Cæsar and Cromwell, in middle age, have snatched all its laurels from opponent commanders bred to it, apparently because capable persons engaged in military pursuits are so scarce that the existence of two of them at the same time in the same hemisphere is extremely rare. The capacity of any conqueror is therefore more likely than not to be an illusion produced by the incapacity of his adversary. At all events, Cæsar might have won his battles without being wiser than Charles XII or Nelson or Joan of Arc, who were, like most modern "self-made" millionaires, half-witted geniuses, enjoying the worship accorded by all races to certain forms of insanity. But Cæsar's victories were only advertisements for an eminence that would never have become popular without them. Cæsar is greater off the battle field than on it. Nelson off his quarterdeck was so quaintly out of the question that when his head was injured at the battle of the Nile, and his conduct became for some years openly scandalous, the difference was not important enough to be noticed. It may, however, be said that peace hath her illusory reputations no less than war. And it is certainly true that in civil life mere capacity for work—the power of killing a dozen secretaries under you, so to speak, as a life-or-death courier kills horses—enables men with common ideas and superstitions to distance all competitors in the strife of political ambition. It was this power of work that astonished Cicero as the most prodigious of Cæsar's gifts, as it astonished later observers in Napoleon before it wore him out. How if Cæsar were nothing but a Nelson and a Gladstone combined! a prodigy of vitality without any special quality of mind! nay, with ideas that were worn out before he was born, as Nelson's and Gladstone's were! I have considered that possibility too, and rejected it. I cannot cite all the stories about Cæsar which seem to me to shew that he was genuinely original; but let me at least point out that I have been careful to attribute nothing but originality to him. Originality gives a man an air of frankness, generosity, and magnanimity by enabling him to estimate the value of truth, money, or success in any particular instance quite independently of convention and moral generalization. He therefore will not, in the ordinary Treasury bench fashion, tell a lie which everybody knows to be a lie (and consequently expects him as a matter of good taste to tell.) His lies are not found out: they pass for candors. He understands the paradox of money, and gives it away when he can get most for it: in other words, when its value is least, which is just when a common man tries hardest to get it. He knows that the real moment of success is not the moment apparent to the crowd. Hence, in order to produce an impression of complete disinterestedness and magnanimity, he has only to act with entire selfishness; and this is perhaps the only sense in which a man can be said to be *naturally* great. It is in this sense that I have represented Cæsar as great. Having virtue, he has no need of goodness. He is neither forgiving, frank, nor generous, because a man who is too great to resent has nothing to forgive; a man who says things that other people are afraid to say need be no more frank than Bismarck was; and there is no generosity in giving things you do not want to people of whom you intend to make use. This distinction between virtue and goodness is not understood in England: hence the poverty of our drama in heroes. Our stage attempts at them are mere goody-goodies. Goodness, in its popular British sense of self-denial, implies that man is vicious by nature, and that supreme goodness is supreme martyrdom. Not sharing that pious opinion, I have not given countenance to it in any of my plays. In this I follow the precedent of the ancient myths, which represent the hero as vanquishing his enemies, not in fair fight, but with enchanted sword, superequine horse and magical invulnerability, the possession of which, from the vulgar moralistic point of view, robs his exploits of any merit whatever.

As to Cæsar's sense of humor, there is no more reason to assume that he lacked it than to assume that he was deaf or blind. It is said that on the occasion of his assassination by a conspiracy of moralists (it is always your moralist who makes assassination a duty, on the scaffold or off it), he defended himself until the good Brutus struck him, when he exclaimed "What! you too, Brutus!" and disdained further fight. If this be true, he must have been an incorrigible comedian. But even if we waive this story, or accept the traditional sentimental interpretation of it, there is still abundant evidence of his lightheartedness and adventurousness. Indeed it is clear from his whole history that what has been called his ambition was an instinct for exploration. He had much more of Columbus and Franklin in him than of Henry V.

However, nobody need deny Cæsar a share, at least, of the qualities I have attributed to him. All men, much more Julius Cæsars, possess all qualities in some degree. The really interesting question is whether I am right in assuming that the way to produce an impression of greatness is by exhibiting a man, not as mortifying his nature by doing his duty, in the manner which our system of putting little men into great positions (not having enough great men in our influential families to go round) forces us to inculcate, but as simply doing what he naturally wants to do. For this raises the question whether our world has not been wrong in its moral theory for the last 2,500 years or so. It must be a constant puzzle to many of us that the Christian era, so excellent in its intentions, should have been practically such a very discreditable episode in the history of the race. I doubt if this is altogether due to the vulgar and sanguinary sensationalism of our religious legends, with their substitution of gross physical torments and public executions for the passion of humanity. Islam, substituting voluptuousness for torment (a merely superficial difference, it is true) has done no better. It may have been the failure of Christianity to emancipate itself from expiatory theories of moral responsibility, guilt, innocence, reward, punishment, and the rest of it, that baffled its intention of changing the world. But these are bound up in all philosophies of creation as opposed to cosmism. They may therefore be regarded as the price we pay for popular religion.